ARCHAEOLINGUA

Edited by
ERZSÉBET JEREM and WOLFGANG MEID

Series Minor
15

ESZTER BÁNFFY

A UNIQUE PREHISTORIC FIGURINE OF THE NEAR EAST

BUDAPEST 2001

This study was supported by the Research Support Scheme (RSS)
of the Soros Open Society Foundation and
the Museum of Fine Arts, Budapest

Cover illustration: Prehistoric figurine of the Near East
from the collection of the Museum of Fine Arts

ISBN 963 8046 36 8
HU-ISSN 1216-6847

2001

ARCHAEOLINGUA ALAPÍTVÁNY
H-1250 Budapest, Úri u. 49

Translated by Magdaléna Seleanu
Graphics: Sándor Ősi
Word processing by the author
Desktop editing and lay-out by András Kardos

Printed by Amulett '98 KFT Budapest

Contents

JOHANNI GEORGIO SZILÁGYI
MAGISTRO HONORATISSIMO

Introduction

And now what hast thou to do in the way of Egypt, to drink the waters of Shihor?
Or what hast thou to do in the way of Assyria, to drink the waters of the River?
(Jeremiah 2: 18)

A clay female figurine was acquired by the Collection of Antiquities of the Museum of Fine Arts in Budapest together with several other Egyptian antiquities from a collection assembled in Egypt. At first glance this object, kept as a permanent deposit in the museum, could not be linked to any known prehistoric or other culture, this being the reason that it had not been exhibited. The figurine has not yet been analyzed or studied in detail and it had also been suggested that the piece might be a fake.[1] One of the principal goals of this study was to either clear the figurine of this suspicion or, if that proved impossible, to confirm that it was indeed a fake. Thus, in addition to its date and probable place of manufacture, I also tried to gather as much information as possible on the historical context in which this and other comparable figurines had been made. What was the meaning and function that this figurine held in its prehistoric settlement or burial ground? How can it be interpreted and into what religious context can it be fitted? The aim of the present study was to gather additional data also on these issues.

The task was also interesting in terms of methodology: would it be possible to draw any conclusions on the historical background, in addition to the description of the figurine's typological features and the search for possible parallels? Could one avoid arguments based on a fragile chain of tentative assumptions? While researching this enigmatic, but significant figurine from the Collection of Antiquities, I experienced both the joys of discovery and a healthy dose of scholarly scepticism.

---

[1] This study grew out of an article intended for the *Bulletin* of the Museum of Fine Arts in Budapest. Its publication was eventually rejected owing to its length. Since, however, my colleagues working in the Antique Department of the Museum of Fine Arts enthusiastically encouraged my work, they generously contributed to its publication. I would here like to thank Prof. János György Szilágyi, the emeritus director of the Collection of Antiquities who, several years ago, first asked me to publish some of the finds in that collection; Dr. Árpád Miklós Nagy, the present curator of the collection, who graciously allowed the publication of the figurine; and, finally, Prof. László Török, my colleague in the Archaeological Institute for his encouragement and help.

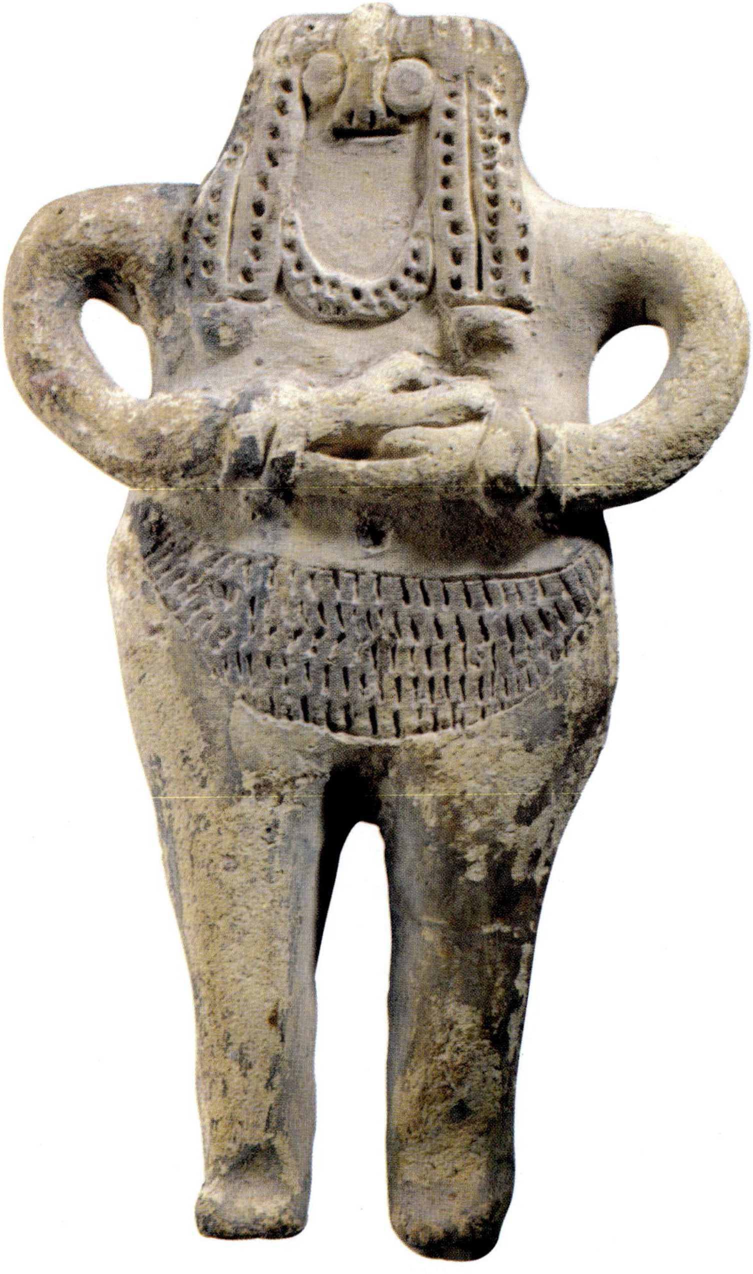

Fig. 1. The whole figure taken from frontside.

Description of the figurine

The figurine, made from yellowish clay mixed with marl, is 16.4 cm high. Small patches of a thin, greyish-brown slip survived on the abdomen and legs. Patches of surface encrustation could be noted on the slightly concave back. These patches always cover the slip. One side of the figurine is more worn: not only has the slip disappeared, the yellow clay surface also shown signs of wear, similarly to the top of the head. The patches of surface encrustation are denser here. It would seem that the figurine had lain with this side upward, more exposed to fluctuations in temperature and humidity.

The remains of black painting can be made out on top of the head, between the hair braids, as shown by four small black patches among the braids near the left ear. The two pupils were most certainly accentuated with reddish-brown paint. The remains of a similar painting can be noted on the hands.

The body of the female figurine is flat, its average thickness does not exceed 1.6–1.7 cm. Aside from the carefully modelled hair braids falling down the back, the backside is not modelled, resembling an almost relief-like depiction. The head is essentially a rectangle joining the body without a neck. The nostrils of the long ridge nose are also indicated, while a deeply incised simple straight line marks the mouth. The eyes of the figurine are rather peculiar: two small applied discs highlighted with painting, covering the better part of the cheeks and giving the impression that the figurine was goggle-eyed. The head is framed with two braids or free-hanging hair, with nine similar braids or locks on the backside. A series of impressed dots, perhaps symbolizing braiding or unruly curls, runs down these locks. A slight protuberance, resembling a headband can be noted at the junction of the brow and the hair, while the nose continues in a similar protuberance on the crown of the head up to the braids falling down to the back of the figurine. These two protuberances might be interpreted as a hair ornament, although this possibility is contradicted by the fact that its surface treatment does not differ from other parts of the head. Densely incised lines cover the crown of the head. These lines can perhaps be taken as indicating the continuations of the braids. Discs ornamented with incised lines can be seen on either side of the head in place of the ears. If the incisions covering the head are interpreted as marking the beginning of the braids, we may say that the way of how these discs covering the ears were worn is not indicated.

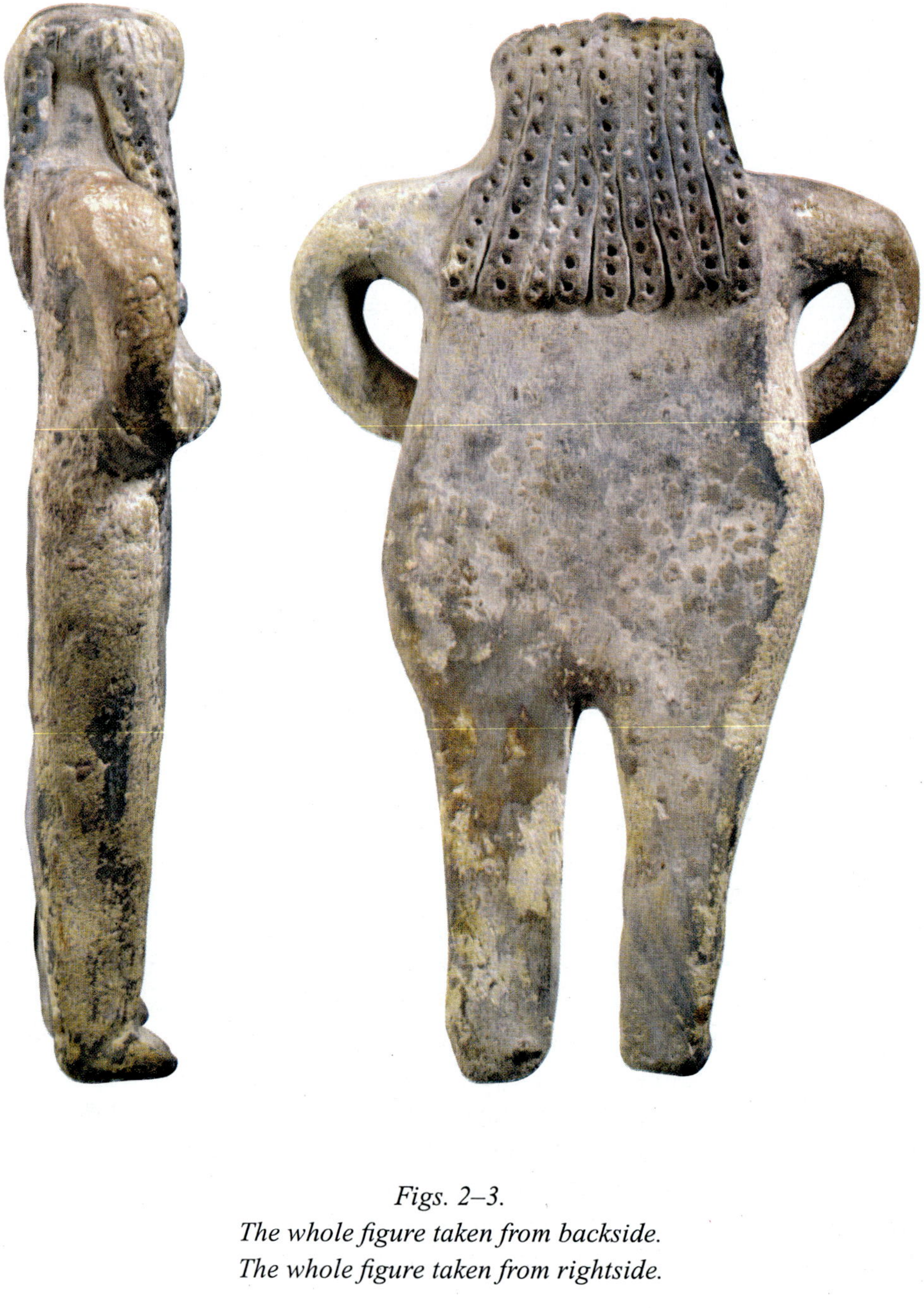

Figs. 2–3.
The whole figure taken from backside.
The whole figure taken from rightside.

The flat, almost two-dimensional body is rather obese, but unmistakably female. Even compared to the wide waist, the broadening hips are emphatically female. The pubic hair, highlighted with five rows of oblique hatching, is set within two arcs under the strongly impressed navel. In contrast, the breasts are rather small compared to the body and they are in part covered by the hair braids. The cylindrical legs of the figurine are separately modelled and are short relative to the overall body proportions. The flat soles enabled the figurine to be set on its feet, even though it could not stand upright unsupported. On one of the feet, the toes are marked with incisions, the other foot is broken.

The posture and arm position of the idol is especially interesting. The cylindrical arms are bent and rest on the abdomen above the navel. The left hand, shown with its palm turned upward, lightly supports the wrist of the right hand that is slightly raised, but does not touch the breast.

Finally, a few words about the jewellery of the idol. The necklace around the neck is modelled similarly to the hair braids: the applied strip of clay is marked with impressed dots. The maker of the figurine perhaps had a necklace of twisted strands or one made up of small links in mind. The wrists are adorned with a pair of rather heavy plain bracelets (semi-circular in section). These bracelets have no ornamentation, no incised or impressed pattern of any kind, and we may therefore assume that they were modelled on bone or shell (perhaps Spondylus) ornaments. In view of the broad spatial and chronological distribution of the figurine, to be discussed below, it is also possible that they depicted ivory bracelets.

To the best of my knowledge, these typological features do not occur together on any figurine published to date. Still, this female figurine has much in common with certain idol types of the Near and Middle East from the 3rd and early 2nd millennium BC. Its classification is complicated by this very fact since the analogous finds show a broad spatial and temporal distribution. Certain typological traits can be found over a rather extensive area, as far away as the Nile Delta in Egypt, through Syria and northern Mesopotamia to the Caspian littoral and the Baluchistan Mountains, the earliest distribution of the Indus valley civilization.

The chronological distribution of comparable idols ranges from the entire 3rd millennium to the early 2nd millennium BC. This period of over a thousand years, however, can be narrowed, considering that the overwhelming majority of comparable figurines which can be precisely dated come from the late 3rd millennium and – more rarely – from the early 2nd millennium BC. Only in the case of idols from an uncertain or inadequately observed archaeological context do we find a general date in the 3rd millennium. Obviously, this cannot be taken to mean that finds comparable to the Budapest figurine were produced and used from the very beginning of the 3rd millennium or throughout its entire span. Its typological and, no doubt, spiritual antecedents are most likely rooted in the Late Neolithic, in the figurines of the Zagros Mountains, northern Mesopotamia and southern Anatolia.[2]

It therefore seems prudent to assess the individual typological features of the idol in a chronological and, more importantly, spatial context, rather than the idol *per se*. Obviously, this can only be the first part of the study, its starting point. Methodologically the most appropriate approach seems to be the study of not only one or the other typological characteristic and its possible parallels, but of as many features as possible.[3] The comparison of these features will hopefully lead to the isolation of a more limited geographical area and a better-circumscribed period of time in which the idol was probably produced. Following the clarification of these questions we must also examine whether these diverse cultural influences could in fact have existed – then and there – as well as the nature of these influences, and the historical and religious context in which this idol had been manufactured and used.

It is equally important to examine the find circumstances and archaeological contexts of comparable figurines. This latter task, however, is encumbered on several counts: many of the idols found before World War II have no archaeological context – if they originate from an excavation at all. The few exceptions include the Ubaid period figurines from cemeteries and graves, but even these often lack an adequate documentation.[4] Unfortunately, only some of the currently known figurines can be linked to a specific site, and very rarely are we told anything about the find circumstances.[5]

---

[2] Broman 1958; Helck 1971.

[3] For an important caveat on methodological difficulties, cf. Ucko 1968, p. 390.

[4] Ucko 1968, p. 440.

[5] I have since learnt that a number of idols have been uncovered in the course of more recent excavations in Syria. These finds, however, are still unpublished. Kind personal communication from Dr. Gábor Kalla.

Typological features

I examined the following typological features of the Budapest idol:

(1) Standing posture, flat body; size
(2) Fabric, painting
(3) Separately modelled legs, differentiated feet
(4) Angular head; vertical applied nose; round applied eyes
(5) Head ornament, applied braids, necklace and bracelets
(6) Arm position
(7) Breasts, navel, depiction of the pubic area; nudity

(1) Standing posture, flat body; size

From the very beginning of the Late Neolithic in the Near East, idols were depicted either standing or sitting – earlier postures appear to be have been discarded. The sitting posture can be linked to the Halaf tradition; standing idols were much more common.

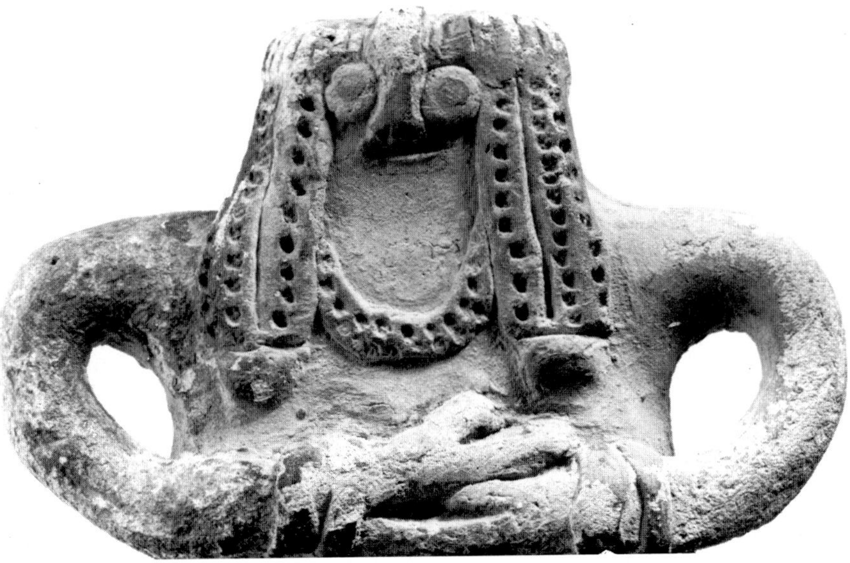

Fig. 4. From the head to the arms.

The fact that the idol is flat is an even more characteristic feature since this strips the figurine of its materiality. Sculpture in the round, if made from clay, was more likely to have been three-dimensional. We must therefore presume a model made from some other fabric. Since bronze was already known in the 3rd millennium BC (a period well into the Early Bronze Age), it seems possible that flat figurines similar to the Budapest one were clay copies of statuettes made from some more valuable metal, such as bronze. However, flat bronze figurines of metal are not known from any of the possible areas or periods,[6] and the few known metal statuettes from the 3rd millennium represent other types.[7] The forerunners of the flat idols are the so-called violin shaped figurines of the Neolithic and the Copper Age which were carved from stone and marble. The fashion of flat depiction spread not only eastwards, but also to the north and northeast during the 4th millennium, i.e. during the South-East European Copper Age. Disregarding now the similar South-East European and well-known Cycladic depictions,[8] comparable violin shaped idols can be quoted from various 4th millennium sites in Asia Minor and Palestine.[9]

Flat depictions both in stone and clay became widespread both in the Near and the Middle East during the 3rd millennium BC. On the testimony of the finds, the traditions of the eastern Mediterranean spread along the southern Pontic littoral to the Caucasus and even beyond the Caspian, to the territory of eastern Iran and southwest Turkmenia.[10] Skirting the Iranian plateau from

---

[6] Human figures of embossed sheet bronze only appeared in the 1st millennium BC. Cf. KELLNER 1982.

[7] Such as the stray find from Horoztepe, Hasanoğlan in the Archaeological Museum of Ankara (inv. no. 13922). The same conclusion can be drawn from the publication of the Mesopotamian and Syrian bronze figurines. Cf. SEEDEN 1980; BRAUN – HOLZINGER 1984.

[8] MONAH 1997, Chapter 7 and the accompanying figures; RENFREW 1977, pp. 59–70; HÖCKMANN 1977, pp. 173–187.

[9] For example from Beyçesultan and the Teleilat Ghassul site of the Ghassul-Beersheva culture of Palestine, dated to the mid-3rd millennium: LLOYD – MELLAART 1966, p. 266, Pl. 32. 1; PERROT 1979, p. 149, Fig. 109.

[10] ANTONOVA 1977, pp. 65–77, Pl. 59 and Figs 63. 2 and 66. 1–7, 9; MASSON – KOROBKOVA 1989, pp. 62–70; SCHMIDT 1937. Several flat idols made from stone have been reported from layer III of Hissar: *op. cit.*, Pl. 45; metal jewellery was placed in the pierced ear of one stylized figurine (no. H 3500).

the south, flat idols also appear to its southeast: the statuette from Tepe Yahya offers a link to the early clay idols of the earliest civilization of the Indus valley.[11]

One of the figurines from the eponymous site of the Halaf culture in Mesopotamia – a flat figurine with hair braids falling down to the back and similar body proportions[12] – can be regarded as a transition between the violin shaped figurines and the type represented by the Budapest figurine.

Most of the currently known flat figurines of the 3rd and early 2nd millennium come from Iraq and Syria. Together with other features, the flat clay body occurs continuously from the Ubaid period to the Early Dynastic period.[13] Such figurines are especially frequent in northern Mesopotamia and along the Syrian coast.[14] The idols from the fortified settlement of Tell Ašmar can also be assigned to this type, as can a flat marble figurine and a few alabaster figurines.[15] The contemporary Khafaje site too yielded similar clay and alabaster idols.[16] The single figurine which can be precisely dated comes from Tell Ašmar: A. Parrot dated it to the 21st century BC.[17] A similar idol from Susa and a stray find from "northern Mesopotamia" was similarly dated

---

[11] LAMBERG – KARLOVSKY 1986, p. 186 and Figs 7. 17, 7. 29; ANTONOVA 1977, Fig. 54. 2 (although Antonova mistakenly described this idol as a male figurine); PIGGOTT 1950, p. 108, Fig. 9, p. 127, Fig. 16; MELLINK – FILIP 1974, Fig. 101.a–c. For the western relations of the Zhob valley, northern Baluchistan and the earliest Indus valley civilization, cf. GAJJAR 1971.

[12] M. OPPENHEIM 1931, Fig. 56. 6.

[13] BURNEY 1977, p. 55; MELLINK – FILIP 1974, Fig. 66.

[14] A comparable flat depiction is a hollow figurine from Yarim Tepe: MUNČAEV – MERPERT 1981, p. 252, Fig. 98. Cf. also MUNČAEV – MERPERT 1981, p. 41, Fig. 11. M. Mallowan has published similar flat idols from the 3rd millennium settlements at Nimrud and Chagar Bazar: MALLOWAN 1947. Five flat idols found at Tell Taya have similarly been dated to the late 3rd millennium: READE 1971, p. 25, Fig. c; READE 1973, pp. 155–158. Comparable idols, made from marble, are known from layer VI of Tepe Gawra: SPEISER 1935, Pls 63–64. Speiser notes that the clay terracotta figurines have little dating value since they were in use over a long period of time.

[15] FRANKFORT 1934, p. 44.

[16] FRANKFORT 1934–35, pp. 70 and 72–73.

[17] PARROT 1962, Fig. 300.

to the close of the 3rd millennium BC.[18] H. Bossert dated five comparable idols from northern Syria and the city of Hama on the Orontes to the turn of the 3rd and 2nd millennium.[19] A terracotta female figurine from the Larsa period, i.e. the turn of the 3rd and 2nd millennium BC, is a close parallel of the Budapest figurine not only as regards its body proportions and arm position, but also in terms of its applied jewellery, hair ornaments, round eyes and nose depiction. The only difference is that this piece, part of the British Museum collection, is a relief.[20] The number of similar female figures, depicted in relief, shows a marked increase from this period.

It must here be noted that this type of depiction can perhaps be associated with the figurines' function. In contrast to a major group of early figurines which, on the testimony of their three-dimensional modelling and the traces of wear on them, were used as part of some kind of (ritual) activity,[21] the Budapest idol and the similar figurines, made to be viewed from *en face*, can be better imagined as set in a separate area inside a dwelling house or a sanctuary. In the latter case they were, together with other cult objects, probably part of a sacral assemblage intended for viewing.[22] It is, however, equally possible (and not only owing to the flat modelling of the body) that these figurines were made for a specific occasion, such as a burial. Although nothing certain can be presumed about the use of a stray find, other possible contexts of use will be discussed at greater length below.

Later depictions of Astarte can be interpreted as the continuation of the flat depictions. These are usually two-dimensional, plaque-like figures or actual plaques.[23]

The dimensions of individual finds are rarely specified in the publications, and the scale is very often unsuitable for determining the size of these figurines. In the case of fragmentary finds even an estimate is often impossible.

---

[18] AMIET 1977, p. 418, Fig. 430.

[19] BOSSERT 1951, p. 43, p. 193, Nos 628, 629 (two pieces), 630 and 631.

[20] CHAMPDOR 1964, Fig. 70.

[21] BÁNFFY 1990–91, Chapter 3.3, with further literature.

[22] For a recent overview of these Late Neolithic and Early Bronze Age assemblages from Greece, cf. MARANGOU 1992, pp. 219–224.

[23] Ten such flat plaques, or their fragments, bearing a depiction of Astarte have been published by ALBRIGHT 1949, pp. 104–106, Fig. 27.

The idols whose sizes are known are all higher than 10 cm, but usually smaller than 22 cm; most have a height ranging between 13 and 18 cm.[24] The size of the Budapest figurine (16.4 cm) corresponds to the idol finds of the 3rd millennium.

It follows from the above that the idol cannot be placed or dated more closely on the basis of these three features (standing posture, flat body and size).

(2) Fabric, painting

The yellowish-whitish-light brownish clay from which the figurine was formed indicates that it had been mixed with marl. Aside from two tiny pebbles, there is no indication that the clay had been tempered. A little non-micaceous sand may have been added to the clay, but it is equally possible that marl acted as the tempering agent. Very little is said about the fabric of the Near Eastern idols in their publications and we therefore have to rely on the better quality photos in this respect. The Budapest figurine does not seem to differ from the published idols of the late 3rd millennium or the turn of the 3rd and 2nd millennium BC. In terms of its surface finish it can be assigned to the same category as household pottery. Still, the carefully smoothed and slightly polished slip no doubt improved its appearance. Considering, however, the art of both Mesopotamia and Egypt from the same period, this idol must be set in a 'rural' context and seen as the work of a local craftsman.

In its present form the idol is light yellow. A closer look reveals that the remains of a greyish-brown slip can be noted on the abdomen and on the legs. This slip was made by immersing the finished clay object in a vessel filled with clayey water before firing. The remnants of this slip that can be noted on various parts of the idol regardless of body part and the usual technique of making a slip suggest that this light brown slip had originally covered the entire surface of the idol. It was also customary to polish vessels covered with

---

[24] Suffice it here to quote the specimens from Tell Halaf (M. OPPENHEIM 1935, No. 122: 14.5 cm; No. 129: 13.6 cm; No. 104: 18.8 cm; the reconstructed height of one of the violin shaped figurines from this site is 15 cm); northern Syria (unprovenanced find dated to the 3rd millennium: DANNHEIMER 1985 (ed.), No. 42: 16.3 cm, No. 44: 10 cm); two idols of the Habuba Kabira type from the 3rd millennium (21.5 cm and 24 cm, resp.); Yarim Tepe (the idol from this site, mentioned in the above, is 19.5 cm high: MUNČAEV – MERPERT 1981, p. 252, Fig. 98).

a slip before firing. This seems to have been the procedure in the case of the Budapest figurine too, and even though the surviving patches of the slip are rather worn, the traces of polishing can be seen and felt.[25]

Traces of black painting can be made out on the head and between the hair braids. This is all the more noteworthy since the paint could be expected to survive better between the incised and stroke-ornamented hair locks than on the plain body parts which were more likely to become worn. The conspicuously worn painting which has survived in much poorer condition than the paint on other parts of the idol suggests that the black paint on the hair was applied after firing. Pastose painting differs from painting applied before firing not only in its technique, but also in terms of the visual effect.[26] One result of the differing painting technique is that as soon as pastose painting comes into contact with water or is rubbed, the painting disappears. Additionally, pastose painting gives a dull effect, differing from paint applied prior to firing. In its original state the black locks of the Budapest figurine gave a more realistic impression than the light brown, shiny skin. Traces of similar black painting have been noted between the locks of the terracotta figurines from Tepe Gawra.[27]

The two pupils were accentuated by brownish-red painting, and traces of a similar painting can be noted on the hands. The painting of the eye made the round applied eyes even more emphatic and no doubt rendered the figurine even more life-like with its 'piercing' stare. Very little can be said about the painting of the hands. It is uncertain to what extent it differed from the light

---

[25] Usually very little is said about possible remains of painting, slip, burnishing or polishing. The reference card of the idol housed in the Brooklyn Museum mentions that this figurine – which stands closest to the Budapest figurine – bears traces of painting. Courtesy of the Brooklyn Museum of Art.

[26] Prehistoric vessels ornamented with painted patterns applied after firing could never be cleaned (either with water or sand). Prehistorians therefore usually consider these Neolithic and Copper Age vessels to have been cult, rather than domestic vessels. However, the pastose painted wares, recovered primarily from Late Neolithic tell settlements – distributed from the Greek isles to the Carpathian Basin – often amount to as much as thirty per cent of the entire ceramic material. The presence of such a large amount of cult vessels on the one hand, and the lack of domestic cooking vessels on the other, seems most unlikely in prehistoric households. Cf. Alram – Stern 1996, Chapter III. 3; Kalicz – Raczky 1984, pp. 85–136.

[27] Tobler 1950, Vol. II, Pl. 81. b, d.

brown slip symbolizing the body. Even though the difference is conspicuous, there is no evidence whatsoever whether hand painting or tattooing using red ochre was practised at the time. The paint remains on the hands could be interpreted as reflecting this practice, but it is equally possible that reddish-brown hands had some actual meaning for the maker of the figurine and his environment – a meaning which remains unknown to us.

In sum, the observations made on the fabric, the quality and the colour of the figurine suggest that the impression made by the figurine differed in antiquity and today. Before we imagine a dreadful creature connected to death based on the figurine's current pale, whitish-yellow colour and clay coloured hair – an all too easy conclusion in view of our imagination honed on bone idols and lekythoi placed in graves – we have to recall that the figurine looked entirely different when it had been made: a female body glowing with health, with the usual colourings of the eastern Mediterranean population: light brownish skin, brown eyes and dark hair.

(3) Separately modelled legs, differentiated feet

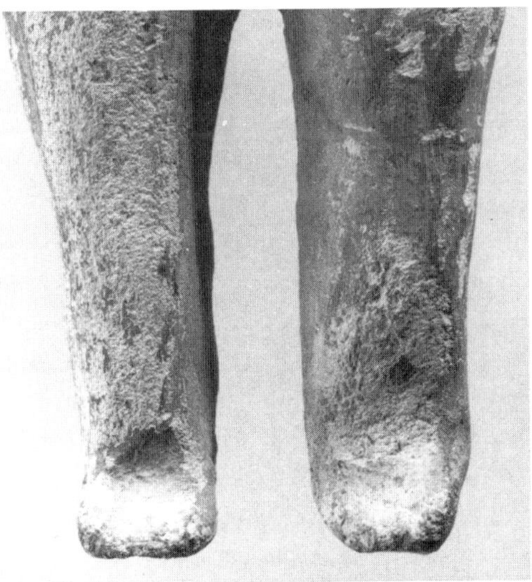

Fig. 5. Legs.

It would appear that the canonization of female figurines at the turn of the 3rd and 2nd millennium did not extend to the modelling of the legs. Although the separation of the legs is always indicated, in many cases this was done by simply incising a vertical line. On Syrian relief depictions the separation of the feet is always indicated for nude female figures.[28] The oft-published idols from Tell Ašmar, dated to the 21st century BC, too have separately modelled legs.[29] An idol with separately modelled legs has also been published from Tepe

[28] Champdor 1964, Figs. 70 and 74.

[29] H. Müller-Karpe 1974, Pl. 206. 27.

Yahya.[30] In view of the latter idol we may perhaps assume an eastern origin, or at least a wide eastern distribution, for separately modelled or separated legs. The closest parallel to the Budapest idol is a figurine with separately modelled legs, exhibited in the Brooklyn Museum of Art, from "Syria, 2200–2000 BC".

We may therefore conclude that this is the least useful stylistic feature since the separation of the legs appears to be the least distinctive trait. Comparable depictions are known from both Syria and Central Asia; at the same time, the separation of the legs is often simply indicated with an incised line, suggesting that the two feet were rarely depicted as being separate. In view of the numerous, incised depictions one could assume that the separation of the legs is the single element which does not harmonize with the otherwise uniform stylistic traits of the statuette. This reservation, however, can be discarded in view of the Syrian idol exhibited in the Brooklyn Museum of Art. Although the separate depiction of the legs does not offer any anchors for a more precise spatial and chronological classification of this find, it does not exclude a Syrian or Palestinian origin.

(4) Angular head; vertical applied nose; round applied eyes

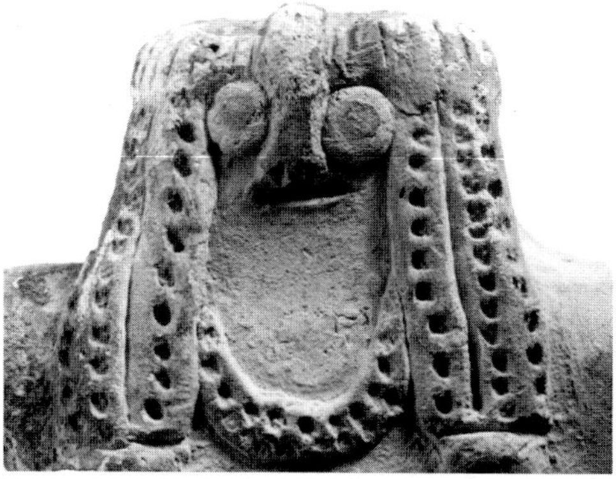

Fig. 6. The head taken from frontside to the end of the tresses and the necklace.

The round applied eyes and the vertical oval piece of clay indicating the nose is one of the most distinctive features of the idol. The plastic eyes were often further accentuated with dark painting and with impressed dots marking the pupils in 3rd millennium Syria.[31] At the same time, the angular head is less common in the eastern and northeastern region, being more widespread in northern Mesopotamia: northern Syria and the eastern Mediterranean.[32]

---

[30] LAMBERG – KARLOVSKY 1986, p. 186, Pl. 7. 17, 29.

[31] E.g. READE 1973, pp. 155–158.

[32] BOSSERT 1951, Nos 630–631; AMIET 1977, Fig. 430; GORDON 1938, pp. 85–88, Fig. 10.

The angularity of the head can usually be attributed to the head ornament. Similar applied head ornaments, usually placed on round or conical heads, can be noted on the earliest depictions from the Indus valley and Baluchistan.[33] A figurine from Turang Tepe in northeastern Iran has similar eyes and nose, but its head is round.[34] Proceeding to the west, we find angular heads in 3rd millennium Susa.[35] The best parallels to the head of the Budapest idol can be quoted from Tell Ašmar, Hama and Tell Taya in northern Mesopotamia.[36] These figurines have rectangular heads, the pupils of the applied eyes are accentuated with painting, and the nose is vertical and ridge-like. The mouth is either not indicated or, similarly to the Budapest idol, it is marked with an incised line. Layer J of the Hama site yielded several clay idols, each of which has large round applied eyes, with the pupils painted with dark colours. This type of eye and nose depiction can be noted on all the clay idols recovered from Habuba Kabira, Tell Huera and Tell Bi'a.[37] However, round applied eyes also occur on idols from more southerly territories in the 3rd millennium.[38] Finally, S. Morenz has published an idol from Egypt whose head has parallelly incised lines similar to the Budapest idol.[39]

---

[33] Agrawala 1965, pp. 24–25. Other figurines in this category include the early Kulli figurines (Piggott 1950, Fig. 9) and the idols from the Zhob valley (Bhattacharyya 1971, p. 22).

[34] Porada 1962, p. 35, Fig. 16.

[35] H. Müller-Karpe 1974, Fig. 250.

[36] Gordon 1938, pp. 85–88, Fig. 10; Reade 1973, pp. 155–158. The finds were recovered from Level IX, dated to the late 3rd millennium.

[37] Amiet 1977, Fig. 430; Frankfort – Lloyd – Jacobsen 1940; Parrot 1962, Fig. 300; for the Sam`al site, cf. Klengel 1977, Chapter 1; Dannheimer (ed.) 1985, Fig. 42; Bossert 1951, p. 193, nos 630–631, the incised line indicating the mouth on figurine no. 630 is similar to the Budapest idol.

[38] Beside the metal vessels, grave 18 of Assur yielded an 11 cm high male figurine with similar eyes. Another interesting feature is that copper and bronze earrings had been fitted into the ears of this figurine, similarly to the slightly earlier Copper Age figurines from the Lower Danube. M. Müller-Karpe 1995, 257–352: cf. also M. Müller-Karpe 1990, Fig. 19.

[39] Morenz 1975, Fig. 19, "Berlin, Äg. Sammlung 24.135".

Although the distribution can be slightly narrowed on the basis of the eyes, the nose and the shape of the head, since the eastern and northeastern territories can now be rejected, the possible chronological and spatial distribution is still too extensive.

(5) Head ornament, applied hair braids, necklace and bracelets

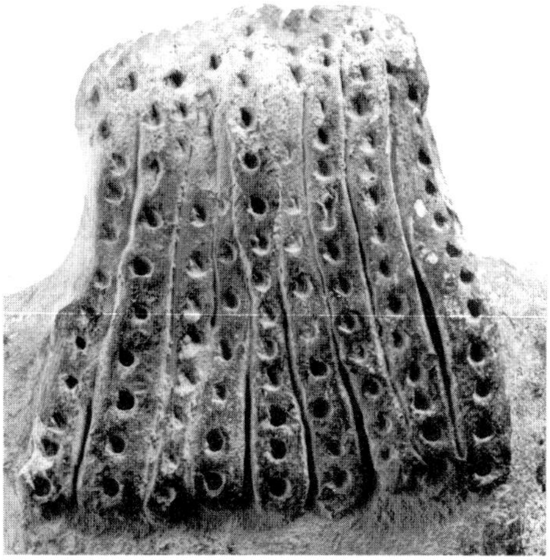

Fig. 7. The head from backside.

Applied discs are usually used to indicate the head ornament or a coiffure of hair locks wound around a hair ornament, while the hair is usually depicted with bundles of incised lines or rows of impressed dots.[40] The earliest example of braids applied to the back of an idol comes from Tell Halaf.[41] This Late Neolithic tradition can later be noted over the entire area, spreading along the northern and southern edge of the Iranian plateau[42] into the early Indus valley civilization, where the early idols of the Kulli, Zhob and Quetta valley all have comparable hair and head ornaments.[43]

Beside the eye, nose and hair depictions, the applied necklaces and bracelets decorated with impressed dots became extremely widespread in northern Mesopotamia and Syria in the late 3rd millennium, and each of the examples quoted in the above could be reiterated here.[44] Most of the idols are

---

[40] The finds quoted in note 24 all have a similar hair ornament.

[41] Several such figurines are known from this site, e.g. M. Oppenheim 1941, Fig. 56.

[42] Cf. the finds from Turang Tepe and other sites in Central Asia, such as Kara Tepe (Masson 1964, Figs 27–28).

[43] Several such finds have been described and published from Kulli, Mundigak IV, Dabar Kot, Quetta–Damb Sadaat and Sur Jangal III. Cf. Chandra 1973; Fairservis 1971; Allchin – Allchin 1968; Dandekar 1969; Gordon 1958.

[44] See notes 26–29; Hrouda 1975, pp. 25–32, Fig. 14, with a date in the later 3rd millennium.

depicted wearing some kind of necklace and, occasionally, also two shoulder straps crossed across the chest, a characteristic trait of the Copper Age and Early Bronze Age of Anatolia and the Near East.[45]

The distribution and type of the bracelets worn by these idols can only be traced with some difficulty, mostly because many of the figurines are broken, and their arms are often missing. There is also evidence that not all of the idols wearing necklaces also had bracelets.[46]

A figurine holding a bowl in the collection of the British Museum also has applied clay hair.[47] On an idol from Gesher, dated slightly later, which has the hands touching the breasts and the abdomen, a highly similar angular ornament marked with incisions can be seen around the head, although this seems to be a new development, symbolizing a head ornament, perhaps a crown, rather than the hair.[48]

The applied braided hair ornament is often associated with the so-called Hathor coiffure of the turn of the 3rd and 2nd millennium BC that – under Egyptian influence – became widespread in certain regions of Syria and northern Mesopotamia, especially in the coastal areas. The female depictions with the coiffure of the Egyptian goddess Hathor are often identified with Astarte, her Mesopotamian counterpart.[49] Analyzing this phenomenon from an Egyptian perspective, W. Helck noted that at the turn of the 3rd and 2nd millennium previously unknown idol types with applied braids made their

---

[45] Beside the figurine from Horoztepe mentioned in the above (see note 5), cf. also AMIET 1977, Fig. 418; BOSSERT 1951, p. 43, no. 628, where the shoulder straps are indicated with incisions. The custom of indicating shoulder straps crossed across the chest can also be noted in the Late Copper Age of the Carpathian Basin. N. Kalicz has aptly noted that these shoulder straps most likely had a unique, but as yet unknown meaning. KALICZ 1981, pp. 235–256, Figs 2–3, 5.

[46] MALLOWAN 1947. The coiffure and the necklace worn by this idol correspond to that on other figurines of this type, their arms are intact and do not sport bracelets.

[47] CHAMPDOR 1964, Fig. 66.

[48] GRESSMANN 1927, Pl. 121. 239.

[49] GRAY 1969, pp. 70–71. This opinion is shared by E. Porada and F. Albright: PORADA 1962, p. 47; ALBRIGHT 1949, pp. 104–106, who notes that the survival of an Early Bronze Age tradition can be assumed for the coiffure depiction of the Astarte figurines from the 2nd millennium.

appearance in Egypt.[50] One excellent example is the angular headed nude female figurine from Egypt published by S. Morenz. The braids frame the head, and cover the neck and the shoulder in three thick braids on the back. The coiffure is indicated with impressed dots. This unprovenanced figurine definitely suggests that this coiffure reached Egypt at a rather early date.[51] Helck attributes the appearance of this idol type to unmistakably Syrian influences.[52]

It would seem that beside the flat body and the above described traits, a coiffure of applied braids was also common to idols of the 3rd millennium, as were necklaces and bracelets (although the latter are not marked with impressed dots). These features seem to indicate the unity of modelling and spiritual content of these idols, rather than revealing additional information about the origins of the Budapest idol.

(6) Arm position

One of the most conspicuous and, at the same time, most intriguing features of the Budapest idol is the position of the arm and hands. The classification of the arm position is rather difficult since in the Near East figurines with arms folded across the breast occur from the Neolithic. The majority of the clay figurines from Hacilar in Anatolia have their arms crossed over the breasts,[53] and this arm position also appears at an early date in Mesopotamia. It is already documented in the Halaf period and it has also been suggested that the crossed arms of the Jarmo figurines can be regarded as a possible precursor.[54] Most of these clay figurines are rather schematic depictions and in many cases the breasts are not indicated separately or perhaps they are covered by the hands resting on them. It is therefore often difficult to distinguish between hands resting on or folded under the breast.

---

[50] HELCK 1971, p. 49. Helck also discusses the possible interpretations of this coiffure, quoting and challenging earlier views (p. 64).

[51] MORENZ 1971, Fig. 19.

[52] HELCK 1971, pp. 48–50.

[53] MELLAART 1961, Figs 11–13.

[54] UCKO 1968, p. 396.

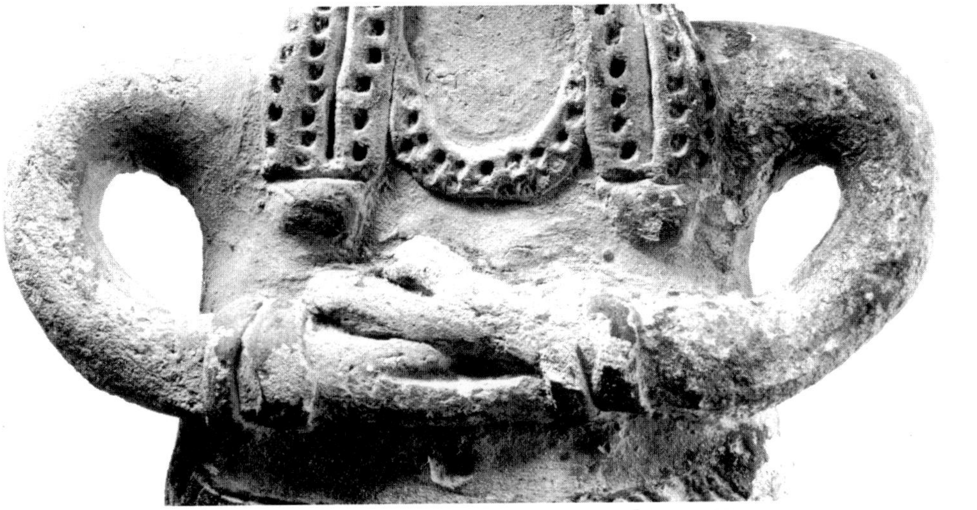

Fig. 8. From the shoulders to the navel.

In many cases it is impossible to reconstruct the arm position of a particular idol since the arms often broke off. Raised arms are characteristic of the 3rd millennium figurines of the Caspian littoral in the northeast.[55] Syrian figurines from the 3rd millennium too often have raised arms, even though these arms are often crudely depicted, as if indicating that although the posture itself is important, the arms as bodily parts are not.[56] The surviving stumps of broken-off arms show a slight curve, suggesting that the arms may have been bent, even though there is no trace of the hands resting on the abdomen.[57]

Hands resting on the breast are not uncommon in the 3rd millennium BC. According to W. F. Albright, the Astarte plaques of the Late Bronze Age have their antecedents in the 3rd millennium BC.[58] This is verified by several

---

[55] PORADA 1962, p. 35, Fig. 62.

[56] BOSSERT 1951, p. 43, nos 628, 630; KLENGEL 1977, Fig. 4; H. MÜLLER-KARPE 1974, Pl. 250. A 3–5, B 1–6, C 3–4. The former come from "Syria, 3rd millennium", the latter were found at Hama on the Orontes.

[57] READE 1973, level IX, late 3rd millennium, and the figures on pp. 155–158. P. Amiet has also published a figurine that compares well with the Budapest idol: AMIET 1977, Fig. 430, a stray find from northern Mesopotamia.

[58] ALBRIGHT 1949, pp. 104–106.

unprovenanced idols from Syria which have the arms crossed under the breasts,[59] as well as by two figurines from well datable contexts.[60] G. F. Dales has noted that in contrast to the type with hands placed onto breasts which has local antecedents, a posture with raised arms is not a local, Mesopotamian development.[61] The occurrence of this arm position in Egypt is similarly attributed to Syrian influences.[62] It is often also uncertain whether the idol has the hands resting on the breasts or whether – in the lack of a separate breast depiction – simply on the chest.[63]

W. Helck proposed an imaginative explanation for the position of the hands resting on or folded under the breast. The so-called eye idols from Brak in northern Mesopotamia are definitely related to Syrian idols, even if this relation is more of an intuition than a typologically documentable relation. According to Helck the conspicuous eyes, whose piercing stare was accentuated by the field between the clay strips, eventually developed into bent arms, and the idol's head must in fact be envisioned above them. The small round breasts between the arms developed from the pupils set within the eyes.[64]

However, the hands resting on the breasts do not correspond with the arm position of the Budapest figurine. The hands are actually resting on the abdomen above the navel. The extended fingers of the left hand support the right wrist, while the right hand almost touches the lower half of the left breast. There are comparable figurines on which the hands are positioned asymmetrically, such as an idol from northern Mesopotamia whose right hand is slightly higher than the left hand supporting it.[65] Comparable flat figurines

---

[59] Dannheimer (ed.) 1985, p. 96, no. 42.

[60] Strommenger 1980, p. 78; Merpert – Munčaev 1981, p. 41, Fig. 11, from Yarim Tepe.

[61] Dales 1960, p. 245.

[62] Helck 1971, p. 50; Contenau 1914, p. 5, Figs 46–47, with the hand resting under the breast on the first idol, and on the breast on the second.

[63] Zettler et al. 1997, p. 31, Fig. 2. One of the figurines has the hands cupping the breast, while on the other the breasts are not indicated, and the hands touch the body in the region of the breasts.

[64] Helck 1971, pp. 20–21. For the eye idols, cf. Goff 1963, pp. 149–151.

[65] Mallowan 1947.

with a hand position similar to the Budapest idol have been found at Nimrud.[66] The bronze female figurines (and the bearded male figures holding maces) found wrapped in cloth at Tell Judeida have been dated to the second half of the Early Bronze Age, the close of the Amuq G period. J. Mellaart has noted that these bejewelled female figurines with their arms crossed across the breast represent a new type in Syria and their appearance coincided with the arrival of new, alien pottery wares.[67] A very beautiful female figure on a relief from Tell Ašmar, dated to the 21st century BC, shows a similar hand position.[68] The clay figurine in the Brooklyn Museum – the closest parallel to the Budapest idol – must also be mentioned here.[69]

The brief typological analysis of the arm position can hardly extend to the meaning or interpretation of individual gestures. It is quite certain, however, that the different arm positions had a symbolic meaning,[70] as indicated by later, written sources and clay figurines recovered from well observed contexts. The symbolic meaning of these gestures, however, still eludes us.

In sum we may say that the occurrence of figurines with an asymmetric arm positions, although not as frequent as specimens with hands resting on the breast or raised arms, can be documented in northern Mesopotamia and Syria. On these idols the right hand is always supported by the left hand. This can hardly be mere chance, again suggesting that the arm and hand position had some concrete meaning for the makers and users of these figurines.

---

[66] Mallowan 1954, pp. 155–163, Fig. 19. 1–7.

[67] Mellaart 1966, pp. 63–64, Fig. 24.

[68] H. Müller-Karpe 1974, Pl. 243.

[69] The description on the reference card reads as follows: "Arms extend outward, bent at elbows, forearms placed one above the other on the body, just beneath the breast, hand without finger delineation." Courtesy of the Brooklyn Museum of Art.

[70] Suffice it here to refer to the Cycladic marble idols with folded arms deposited into graves, or the Cretan figurines with upraised arms holding snakes. The 'supplicant pose' is a concept from classical antiquity that has often been projected back into prehistory. Even P. Ucko, who rejects the idea of canonization in the case of prehistoric idols, notes that "the arms on the breasts or between the breasts would seem to be an unlikely gesture for a woman in the process of childbirth." Ucko 1968, p. 440.

(7) Breasts, navel, depiction of the sexual part; nudity

It would seem that nudity is one of the most distinctive features of prehistoric idols. The female figurines of the Neolithic communities in the Near East, Anatolia, the Aegean, the Balkans and Central Europe are without exception depicted without clothes. The first figurines which are believed to be clothed – an assumption based on the incised patterns covering their body – appeared at the turn of the Late Copper Age and Early Bronze Age on the territory of present-day Croatia, Slovenia and southern Transdanubia. These incised

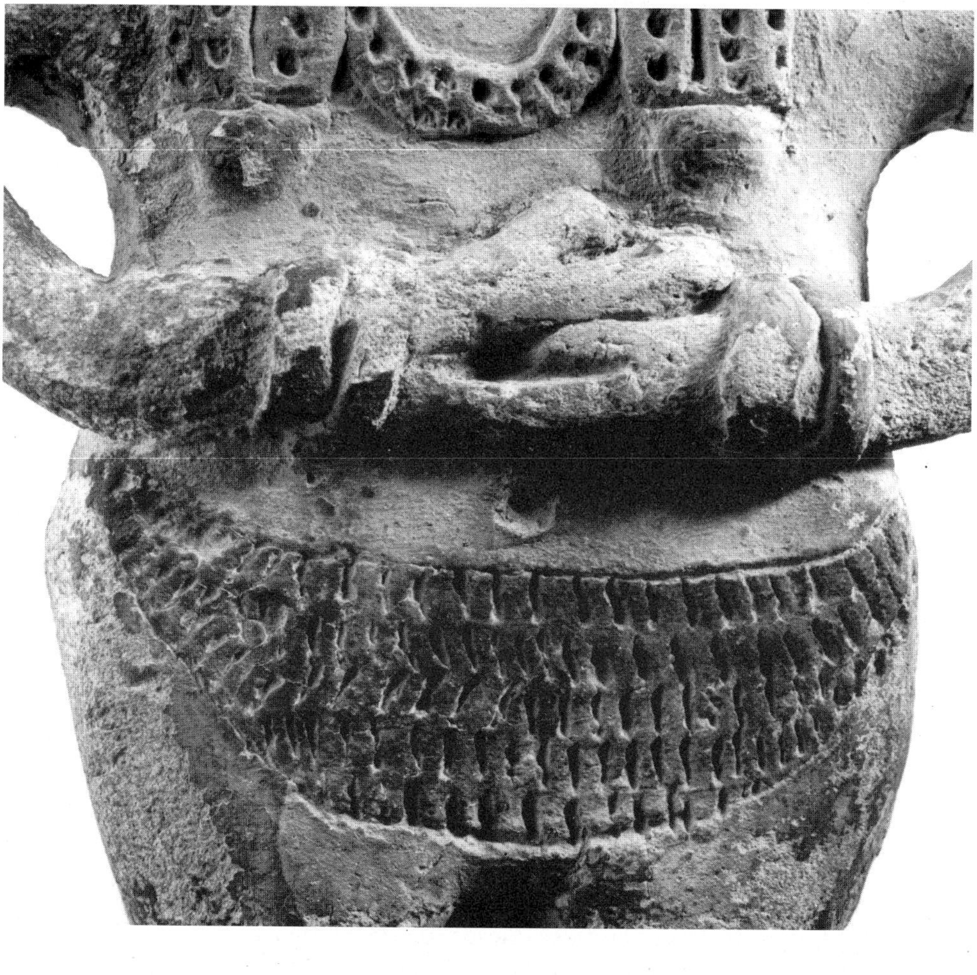

Fig. 9. From the breast to the pubic triangle.

patterns became the basis for the reconstruction of prehistoric clothing.[71] In most parts of Europe human figurines virtually disappeared during the long centuries of the Early Bronze Age and the beginning of the Middle Bronze Age.[72] The few known figurines from the Bronze Age are usually clothed in long skirts or dresses.[73] One group of reliefs from the 2nd millennium in Mesopotamia, interpreted as depictions of Astarte, show the goddess clothed in a long dress and flowing cloak. This depiction type shows the goddess holding a plant in one hand,[74] or with the hand held loosely beside the body.[75]

The late appearance of clothed idols poses two problems. The first is that from the Middle Neolithic there appear idols whose bodies are decorated with incised or painted patterns throughout this vast culture province. The same patterns can be noted on the pottery and, very often, on the house models of these cultures,[76] suggesting that these patterns should not be interpreted as costume depictions. To the best of my knowledge only M. Gimbutas considers these idols to be wearing a 'ritual costume'.[77] Although the idols of the Halaf culture are decorated with painted patterns that usually cover the shoulders, the arms and the legs, these figurines can nonetheless be considered nude depictions.[78] It is equally uncertain whether the cross shaped pattern on the chest of Copper and Bronze Age idols is an indication of clothing or jewellery, perhaps tattooing or body painting, or whether it was a symbol which was associated with the meaning of the idol, rather than its body.

---

71 Schmidt 1945; Benac – Tasić (eds) 1979, Pl. 34. 3–5. Another problem of interpretation is that the body of a bird figurine from this site was dressed in a similar 'clothing' (Pl. 29. 8).

72 Clothed figurines of this type are known from the Iron Gates region and the Lower Danube (Gîrla Mare culture). Cf. Letica 1973.

73 Nilsson 1950, Chapter 2, esp. p. 86.

74 Champdor 1964, Fig. 74, left.

75 M. Oppenheim 1941, Fig. 104.

76 The 'textile patterns' ornamenting the Venus of Kökénydomb and the figurines from Szegvár can also be found on the pottery of the Tisza culture. Cf. Csalog 1959, pp. 7–38. The walls of the house model from Öcsöd are covered with a similar pattern. For one possible interpretation, cf. Bánffy 1986a.

77 Gimbutas 1982, pp. 44–56.

78 For a good overview of the idols of the Halaf culture, cf. Mellaart 1975, Fig. 101. An ornamentation of black painted bands can also be seen clearly on these idols.

The other problem is that – viewing Neolithic sculpture as a whole – it is impossible to ascertain whether the idol is clothed, especially in the case of schematic figurines. The small, indistinct knobs marking the breasts are often only sufficient for indicating the sex of the idol. If the idol does not bear any other incised or painted pattern, it is hard to establish whether the female figure was depicted in the nude or wearing a costume.[79]

In view of the above, one important caveat in the interpretation of Neolithic and Early Bronze Age idols on which nudity is a distinctive trait is that this nudity is far from unambiguous and that its meaning perhaps varied from culture to culture. Fortunately, some figurines – such as the Budapest idol – have certain features on the basis of which we can definitely claim that the idol is nude. One of these features is the indication of the navel. Considering the often scanty clothing of Bronze Age 'clothed' idols,[80] the indication of the navel does not always offer irrefutable proof, but it is a fact that the dress did not cover the abdomen. The navel is usually marked with an impressed round cavity, as on the Budapest figurine.[81] In some cases the navel is applied separately, similarly to the eyes or the links of the necklace, as on an idol from Tell Ašmar.[82] On two Egyptian idols, housed in Berlin, the navel was marked with a series of light impressions.[83] The perhaps most ingenious solution can be seen on a headless idol from Yarim Tepe that has the hands resting on the breasts: the navel is marked with a dark painted rectangle enclosing a four petalled flower.[84]

The depiction of the pubic triangle leaves no doubt as to nudity. Although the idols from the Middle East, i.e. from the settlements along the routes skirting the Iranian plateau from the north and south, and the idols of the early Indus valley civilization in Baluchistan share certain features with the Syrian

---

[79] The majority of the so-called violin shaped idols of the Early Bronze Age can be assigned to this category, as can most of the Cycladic anthropomorphic figurines. Cf. Thimme (ed.) 1977, and Höckmann 1977, pp. 173–185.

[80] I am here thinking of the Cretan female figurines. Higgins 1981, Figs 3 and 22–23.

[81] On the basis of the illustrations, the nude idols published by Bossert can be assigned to this group. Bossert 1951.

[82] Parrot 1962, Fig. 300.

[83] "Berlin Äg. Sammlung 24.135 and 24.136", published by Morenz 1975, Figs 19–20.

[84] Merpert – Munčaev 1981, Fig. 11.

and Mesopotamian figurines, they certainly differ as far as the depiction of the pubic part is concerned. Even though only the heads, the shoulders and the upper parts of most idols have survived, the few intact idols leave no doubt that the lower part of the body is schematic, crude or, occasionally, covered by a dress.[85] One common feature of all clay figurines from northern Mesopotamia and the Syro-Palestinian region is that the pubic part that is disproportionately large and that it is further accentuated with incisions and strong contours.

In northern Mesopotamia the depiction of the pubic area appears in the Ubaid period in 4500 BC, becoming widespread in the Early Dynastic period and surviving throughout the Bronze Age.[86] Such late 3rd millennium figurines have been published by P. Amiet,[87] and several comparable figurines are known from Tell Taya. One of the published illustrations clearly reveals that the sculptor also depicted the vulva with a strongly incised line in the lower half of the pubic triangle.[88] A variant of this depiction of the pubic part can be noted on another figurine from Tell Taya: here the incised line appears within a circle. The pubic part of an idol with raised arms from Hama is similarly circular.[89] A third variant can be noted on a figurine from Tell Ašmar: the pubic hair is incised within a U shaped area.[90] The idols from Tell Ašmar also include specimens with a crudely modelled pubic triangle.[91] A comparable figurine is known from Egypt.[92]

These variants all appear on the Budapest idol: the pubic area appears between two curved lines, the upper line lying a little under the navel and

---

[85] Fairservis 1971, pp. 33, 205, 227; Piggott 1950, p. 108, Fig. 9, unprovenanced. The idol from Kulli is published in profile, but the strongly schematized depiction is obvious even from this view.

[86] Mellink – Filip 1974, Fig. 66; Burney 1977, p. 55.

[87] Amiet 1977, Figs 418 and 430.

[88] Reade 1973, Part 2, pp. 155–158.

[89] Bossert 1951, No. 630.

[90] H. Müller-Karpe 1974, Pl. 206; Frankfort – Lloyd – Jakobsen 1940; Frankfort 1939.

[91] Frankfort 1934. The round shape also occurs among these finds.

[92] A schematic drawing of the idol can be seen on W. Helck's plate of the late 3rd millennium idol types. The find spot is given as "Diospolis parva". Helck 1971, p. 57.

joining with the lower line at the narrow waist. This is not a genuine triangle, although close to it, not a genuine U shaped pubic area, although close to it.

The interior of the pubic area also differs widely. In some cases, it is filled with regularly spaced vertical lines, in some cases with raindrop-like impressed dots and lines.[93] In some cases the anatomical dividing line between the thighs and the abdomen coincides with the lower part of the pubic area and the area marked with the contours is closed off on top with a horizontally incised line under the navel, while the interior is left empty or filled with a few horizontal lines.[94]

Most of the depictions mentioned here suggest that these are not naturalistic portrayals. The pubic area is depicted with deeply incised lines and hatching, and it is disproportionately large. The same holds true for the Budapest idol, where the entire lower part of the abdomen is covered with the pubic area and the pubic hair is indicated with hatching.

The fact that this depiction type has nothing to do with naturalistic portrayal is perhaps most spectacularly illustrated by the pubic triangle on the headless idol from Yarim Tepe. The pubic triangle, bordered by two parallel painted lines and filled with dotting, extends to the feet of the figurine. It is therefore uncertain whether the vertical black line running down about one-fifth of the triangle marks the vulva or the separation of the feet.[95] The two upper tips of the triangle extend to either side of the hips.

The typological features associated with the nudity of the figurine indicate that development in the eastern region took a different path. The closest analogies to the Budapest idol can be quoted from northern Mesopotamia, the Syrian coast and Syria-Palestine as regards the modelling of the breasts, the navel, and especially the pubic area. The depiction of the pubic area on these figurines is most emphatic, both as regards their proportion and their portrayal, and it is tempting to assume that these female figurines were given such wide hips in order to leave ample room for the incised body part marked with contours.

---

[93] Examples can be quoted for both types, often from the same site, e.g. from Tell Taya (cf. note 81). Some scholars believe that the impressed pattern in the pubic area represents rain and its function is none other than "an appeal to the goddess to contribute to the growth of crops". GOLAN 1991, p. 18. One of the idols from the 3rd millennium published here comes from Syro-Palestine.

[94] BOSSERT 1951, Nos 628 and 631.

[95] MERPERT – MUNČAEV 1981, Fig. 11.

Summary of the typological features

The isolation and separate analysis of the typological traits of one individual figurine is not entirely without danger since the very essence may easily be missed among the details during the search for possible analogies. In the case of the Budapest idol this approach seemed necessary because aside from the appearance of the figurine there was no other starting point for determining the place and date of manufacture. Moreover, all similar finds are distributed over a rather extensive area and date to a rather broad period of time. It seemed reasonable to attempt the assignment of individual typological features to a more specific geographic area and chronological horizon in the hope that the sum of these features would outline the place and time of manufacture of the Budapest idol.

This is obviously only a possibility: we may say that of the possible areas of origin Afghanistan and Iran (both southern Iran and the Caspian littoral) can be excluded since the idols from this region differ in the portrayal of the head, the coiffure and the lack of emphasis on nudity. It is also unlikely, for the same reasons, that the figurine had been manufactured in southern Mesopotamia. Although the number of published figurines from this region is conspicuously low, with the illustrations in the publication focusing on the human figures depicted on cylinder seals and on a few carefully modelled figurines. Northern Mesopotamia as a possible place of origin cannot be rejected out of hand, although the arm position of the idols from this region differs: most idols have raised arms. Still, examples of hands folded under the breasts are known from this area.

In view of the head form and the coiffure, the Egyptian connections of the Budapest idol are striking. Portrayals of this type are primarily known from the Orontes region, Hama and Byblos, southern Syria – especially the areas bordering on Palestine – and, more rarely, from northern Palestine. The clay figurine in the Brooklyn Museum of Art that according to its description matches the Budapest idol in all typological features, probably comes from this area.

We may therefore conclude that the separate analysis of the typological traits did yield some results. The eastern region can most certainly be rejected as a possible place of origin, as can southern Mesopotamia. Northern Mesopotamia remains a possible candidate (although with a question mark), but only because the most likely place of origin, the Levant – i.e. Lebanon and Syro-Palestine – cannot be proven one hundred percent. This could only become a certainty if there were well-documented assemblages containing such figurines with known contexts. Until then, no matter how convincing this possibility as the idol's place of manufacture, other possible provenances – such as the Euphrates region in northern Mesopotamia – cannot be dismissed.

The chronological classification of the Budapest idol and its analogies is a simpler task since comparable depictions are without exception dated to the later 3rd millennium (including the figurines of the early Indus valley civilization of Baluchistan). More closely dated finds, such as the finds from Tell Ašmar, are assigned to the 21st century BC, while the figurine in the Brooklyn Museum of Art is dated to the 22nd–20th century BC. The Budapest idol can therefore be assigned to the very end of the 3rd millennium BC, a date that is not contradicted by any other known find.

Although the typological analysis was fruitful, its results raise two additional questions. The – no doubt related – idols with applied eyes and hair and jewellery are distributed over an unusually extensive area, mostly west, north and east of the Mesopotamian centre, on the periphery of the flourishing cities along the lower reaches of the Tigris and the Euphrates. This relationship – if it indeed existed – was probably not only reflected in the manufacture of idols.

The other problem concerns Egypt. The regions bordering on the Syrian littoral had both overland and marine trade contacts with the Nile Delta, even though these trade contacts cannot be demonstrated for all periods. Fortunately, there is a wealth of written evidence from the Old Kingdom and the First Intermediate Period, and several excellent studies on these two periods are also available. The hypothesis based on the typological features must therefore be juxtaposed with the historical evidence: did, or could this contact have existed in the assumed period and place, i.e. in a Syro-Palestinian 3rd millennium context, either through trade, cultural contact or population migrations which would provide an authentic historical context for the diverse typological features on the Budapest idol.

The historical background

(1) Chronology

Although it has little relevance for the Budapest idol or the historical events, the fact that scholarly opinion is divided on the evaluation of the individual phases of the Bronze Age calls for a brief overview of the various opinions on the late 3rd millennium, i.e. the end of the Early Bronze Age or, according to some views, the transition between the Early and the Middle Bronze Age – the period which most likely saw the manufacture of the Budapest idol.

Syro-Palestinian chronology is naturally based on Egyptian chronology, in our case the end of the Old Kingdom which, following Pepi II's long and peaceful reign, can be put at the end of the VIth Dynasty, to the first decades of the 22nd century.[96] In Syria this period corresponds to the end of Amuq (and Hama) J, or to the classical phase of the Amuq J period in Braidwood's scheme, and the latest phase of the Early Bronze Age (EB III). W. F. Albright interpolated an Early Bronze Age IV phase, lasting until 2040 since his EB III (Early Bronze Age C) phase ends in the 24th century. K. Kenyon believed that the transition between the Early and the Middle Bronze Age can be put before 2181 since Syro-Palestine came under the rule of nomadic tribes until 1991, marking the commencement of a new period.[97] Based on a detailed analysis of the pottery finds from various sites and an elaborate system of cross-dating, J. Yakar concluded that the EB IIIa–c lasted from 2400 BC until the end of the millennium.[98]

As a matter of fact, these small differences of chronology are of little importance in terms of the historical events and the Budapest idol. The close of the 3rd millennium corresponds to the final phase of the Early Bronze

[96] This period is dated to 2250 by H. J. Kantor, to 2181 by J. Mellaart and to 2155 by L. Kákosy. Cf. R. E. Ehrich (ed.), *Chronologies in Old World Archaeology*; Kantor 1979, p. 20; Mellaart 1966, p. 71 and the chronological chart; Kákosy 1979, p. 99.

[97] Kühne 1976, pp. 115–117, and the comparative chronological chart on p. 115; Kenyon 1970, p. 159.

[98] Yakar 1985, pp. 330–349, and the chronological chart on p. 333.

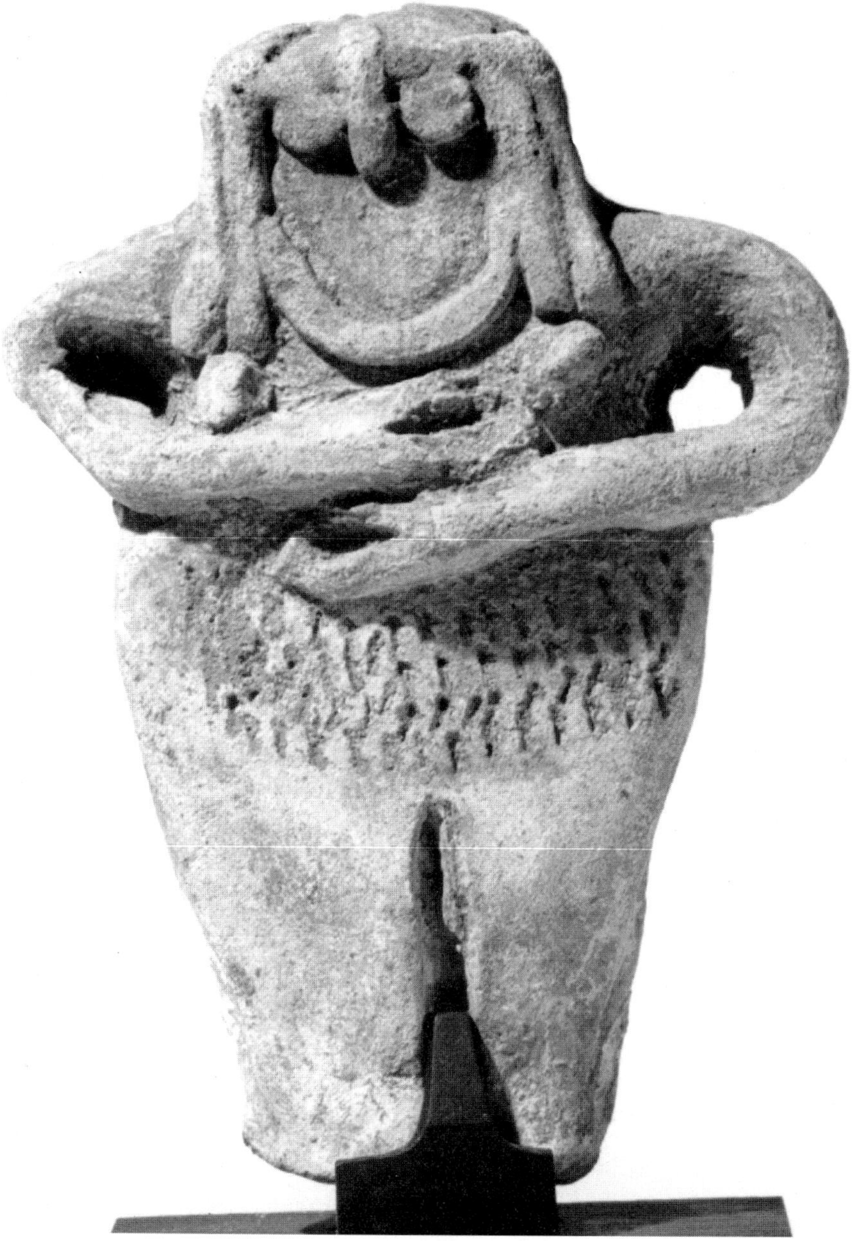

Fig. 10. The Figurine from the collection of the Brooklyn Museum of Art.
Courtesy of the Brooklyn Museum of Art, 72.133.
Gifts of Mrs. Helena Symkovitch in Memory of Vladimir G. Symkovitch.

Age in the cities on the Syrian littoral,[99] and the same holds true for the chronology of the Palestinian settlements. The last dynasties of the Old Kingdom (Dynasties IV–VI) and the commencement of the First Intermediate Period can be assigned to this period. Even if there is a few years' difference in the relative or absolute chronology of the end of the Early Bronze Age, this does not influence relative chronology and the consensus on the instability marking the close of the EBA. Most scholars also agree that these processes can be linked to the close of the 3rd millennium.[100] This period of change and turmoil could be felt not only in Egypt, but also in the Levant, as well as in the inland regions of Syria and Palestine, and it marked the end of the long peaceful centuries of the Early Bronze Age.[101]

It is also quite certain that with the First Intermediate Period, Egyptian trade patterns also changed. Although trade relations with Syria were renewed during the Middle Kingdom, only marine routes were used, and trade was essentially restricted to Byblos. The importance of the overland route vanished completely, and only a few campaigns were led against the inland areas of Palestine, in order to subdue the local tribes. Most scholars agree that these events can be dated to the turn of the 3rd and 2nd millennium and the beginning of the 2nd millennium.[102]

It follows from the above that in spite of smaller differences of opinion, the close of the Syro-Palestinian Early Bronze Age is dated more or less uniformly: according to the Egyptian chronology it can be placed at the end of the Old Kingdom and the close of the First Intermediate Period, i.e. to the period between the VIth–XIIth Dynasties. Although the historical events in southern Mesopotamia had less impact on the development of the investigated area, it must nonetheless be noted that this period coincides with the end of the Sargonid rule and the beginning of the Third Dynasty of Ur.

The Budapest idol was thus probably made sometime during the last centuries of the 3rd millennium, during the period that saw the end of the

---

[99] For a detailed comparative chronology of northern Syrian and Anatolian sites, cf. Parzinger 1993, with further literature.

[100] Mellaart 1979, pp. 6–18. For absolute chronology, cf. Munn – Rankin 1980, pp. 128–129.

[101] Kantor 1992, p. 21; Jidejian 1971, pp. 21–23.

[102] Daumas 1969, pp. 716–718 (chronological charts).

Old Kingdom, the First Intermediate Period and the reign of the VIth–XIIth Dynasties. In Byblos this corresponds to layer VII, while in Palestine, northern Syria and the Amuq plain to the last phase of the Early Bronze Age.

(2) Early Bronze Age development in Syro-Palestine and the eastern region

At the time of the unification of Upper and Lower Egypt, at the beginning of the Old Kingdom, urbanization had already begun in Palestine and the Levant. On the testimony of the toponyms, the spoken language of the region was – in contrast to southern Mesopotamia – a Semitic tongue.[103] Depictions of foreign sailors, perhaps merchants from Byblos, considered to belong to some Semitic tribes – are known already from the time of the Ist Dynasty.[104]

The Syro-Palestinian region had strong ties with the Old Kingdom of Egypt. The Arad settlement, lying among the hills west of the Dead Sea and occupied during the Copper and the Early Bronze Age, yielded the fragment of a jug inscribed with the name of Narmer, the last pre-Dynastic ruler of Egypt, from the EB I layer.[105] The ceramic repertoire recovered from the contemporary 'Canaanite'[106] settlement at Tell Gath was predominantly Egyptian, suggesting that these were not imports, but that the occupants were Egyptian.[107] Another such site was uncovered at nearby Tel Maahaz, where Egyptian wares made up ninety per cent of the pottery, and En Besor, which yielded thirty Egyptian clay bullae bearing impressions of Egyptian cylinder seals from the time of Den. The locally made copy of an Egyptian cylinder seal bearing the depiction of an early Egyptian shrine was found at Gezer in Palestine.[108] This would imply that there were Egyptian towns in Palestine

---

[103] MELLAART 1966, p. 54.

[104] MELLAART 1966, p. 55. According to J. Mellaart, a Semitic language was spoken in Syria, Lebanon and Palestine from with the Late Chalcolithic Period. MELLAART 1966, p. 54.

[105] AMIRAN 1992, pp. 32–33, Fig. 20.

[106] This expression is used mainly by Israeli scholars for the southern Syrian and Palestinian region.

[107] BEN-TOR 1981, p. 449.

[108] BEN-TOR 1981, p. 449.

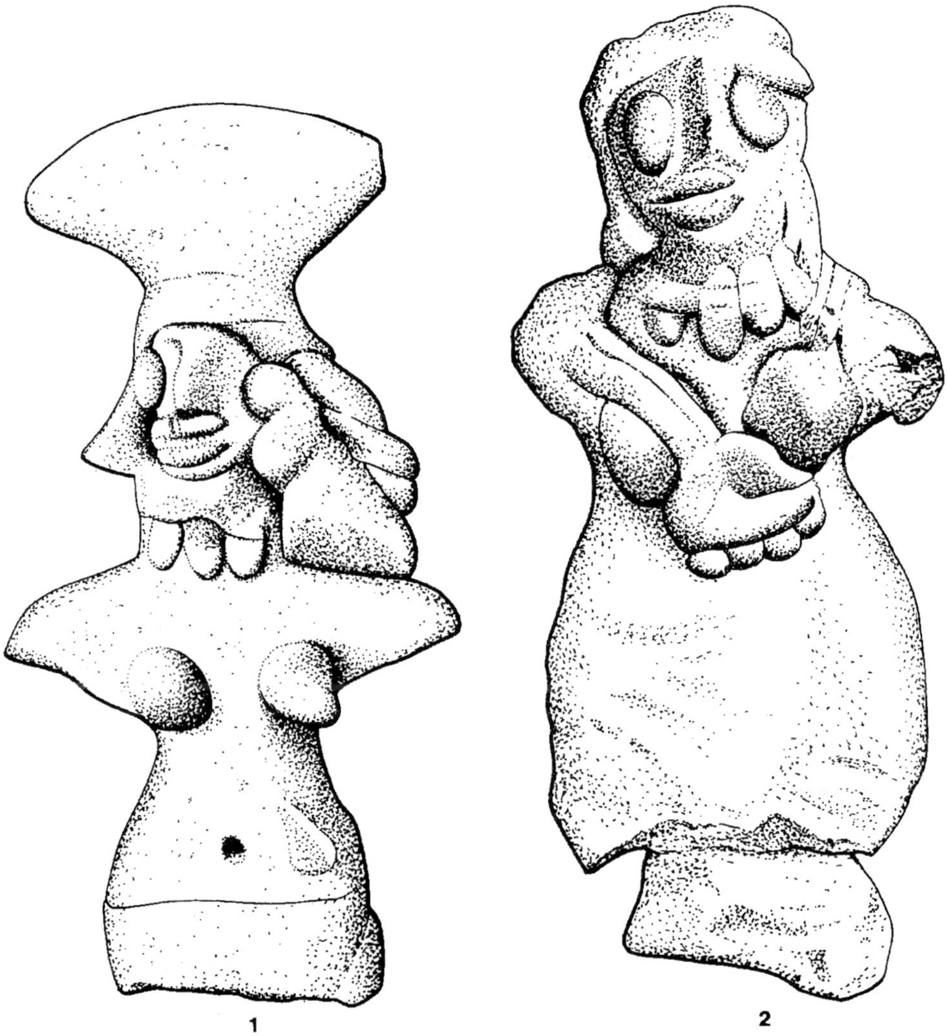

Fig. 11.

1. Indus Valley Civilisation.
Courtesy of the National Museum, New Delhi (DK 1266/264).
2. Indus Valley Civilisation.
Courtesy of the National Museum, New Delhi (H 557/373).

during the Old Kingdom – such as Tel Gath – while elsewhere the local population, speaking a Semitic tongue, moved from the neighbouring villages into the flourishing fortified cities such as Arad.[109]

Egypt maintained lively trade relations with the coastal cities of the Early Bronze Age, and especially with Byblos.[110] The first walled urban settlement (Byblos IV) began to flourish during the Copper Age-Bronze Age transition. Layer V can be dated with stone vases from the Ist and IInd Dynasties. The best preserved Early Bronze Age settlement was uncovered in layer VI. At this time Byblos was an open town: it did not have fortifications as the other towns of southern Palestine, but it had at least three temples, one of which was dedicated to Baalat Gebal, the Lady of Byblos.[111] On the testimony of the inscribed stone vases recovered from this temple, Egyptians also offered sacrifices to the goddess. The latest Egyptian jug bears the stamp of Pepi II, the last ruler of the VIth Dynasty.[112] The finds from Byblos indicate that at the time of the town's flourishing, the sons of many nations visited the town, similarly to any modern sea-port. The hieroglyphic inscription on an obelisk from one the town's temples records that it had been set up in honour of an Amorite prince of Byblos by a man from western Anatolia. The inscription dates from the 21st century.[113]

As the centre of the timber trade with Egypt, Byblos enjoyed a monopoly at this time. Good quality timber – and especially cypress – used in the construction of houses and ships was important for Egypt and this provided the basis of Byblos' wealth.[114] Beside timber, Byblos was also the centre of trade in oil, lapis lazuli and ivory. Lapis lazuli arrived from the east, ivory came from Egypt. Trade flourished in silver from the Zagros Mountains in Iran and in cylinder seals and metal vessels, mostly spouted jugs, from southern Mesopotamia.[115] Locally produced olive oil was traded for alabaster

---

[109] Amiran 1992, p. 95.

[110] Accordingly, major cultural differences can be noted between the coastal and inland areas. Cf. Liebowitz 1972, pp. 95–105.

[111] Mellaart 1966, p. 64.

[112] Mellaart 1966, p. 70.

[113] Mellaart 1966, pp. 71–72.

[114] Mellaart 1966, p. 56.

[115] Perrot 1978, p. 170; Mellaart 1966, p. 56; M. Müller-Karpe 1990, pp. 173–174.

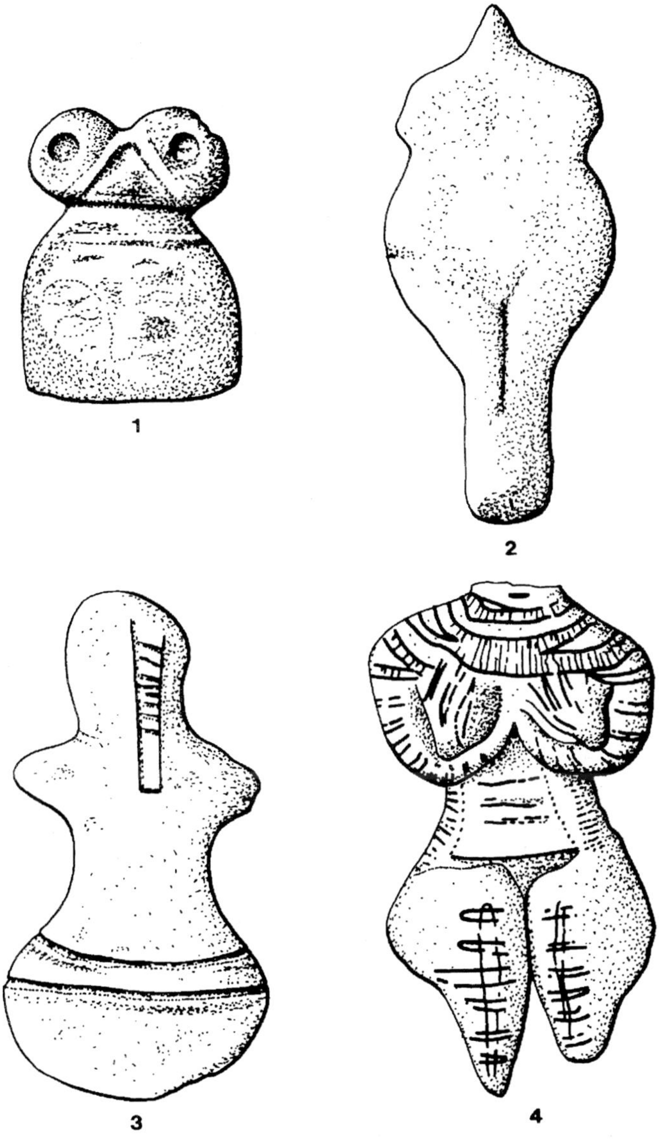

Fig. 12.

1. Braq. (After M*ALLOWAN 1947, Pl. 26/3);*
2. Braq. (After M*ALLOWAN 1947, Pl. 26/7);*
*3. Tell Halaf. (*O*PPENHEIM, Freiherr 1935, Fig. 56/6);*
4. Chagar Bazar/Chabur. (After M*ELLAART 1975, Fig. 101).*

vases and cult objects, including alabaster vases inscribed with the name of Hathor, from Egypt that were then transported to the towns of the Levant.[116] The few Palestinian vessels found in Old Kingdom burials can probably be interpreted as containers, used for transporting olive oil.[117] It seems that idols too arrived to Egypt from the Syro-Palestinian region. And since clay figurines were unknown in the Old Kingdom, their unexpected appearance must be attributed to external influences from the Levant,[118] a fact that harmonizes with what we know about the flourishing trade relations between the two regions.

Two separate trade routes between Egypt and Syro-Palestine, one overland, the other marine, can be distinguished in the Early Bronze Age.

In the second phase of the Early Bronze Age, at the time of the Vth Dynasty in Egypt, the marine route between the Nile Delta and the eastern Mediterranean became increasingly important, as shown by the Egyptian wares in Ebla, lying more inland,[119] and Anatolia, including the northwestern areas. In his discussion of the Dorak hoard, J. Mellaart too invokes these trade connections.[120] Mellaart naturally believes that the hoard is an existing and authentic assemblage.[121] The authenticity of the Dorak hoard is crucial for the chronology of Balkanic-Aegean prehistory. If the Dorak burial had indeed contained the Early Bronze Age objects from Egypt drawn by Mellaart, this could be one of the most important chronological anchors between Egypt with its precise chronology and the recent attempts at 'anchoring' Asia Minor with calibrated radiocarbon dates.[122] Even so, W. Helck has aptly pointed out that

---

[116] Perrot 1978, p. 170.

[117] Ben-Tor 1981, p. 449.

[118] Helck 1971, p. 49.

[119] Bermant – Weitzman 1986, p. 32.

[120] Kantor 1992, p. 21. The much-debated Dorak treasure stirred quite a controversy in the scholarly community. Mellaart only published a drawing of the items in the treasure (Mellaart 1966, Pls 17–18, 22a–b). For an account on the subsequent fate of the treasure, often not unlike a modern crime story, cf. Pearson – Connor 1967.

[121] Mellaart 1966, pp. 128–132.

[122] After reading the book on the Dorak treasure, and in view of J. Mellaart's impeccable and reliable work, it is my conviction that Mellaart did not falsify the truth – a conviction confirmed also by the arm position of the Egyptian idols from the treasure which share a resemblance with that of the Budapest idol.

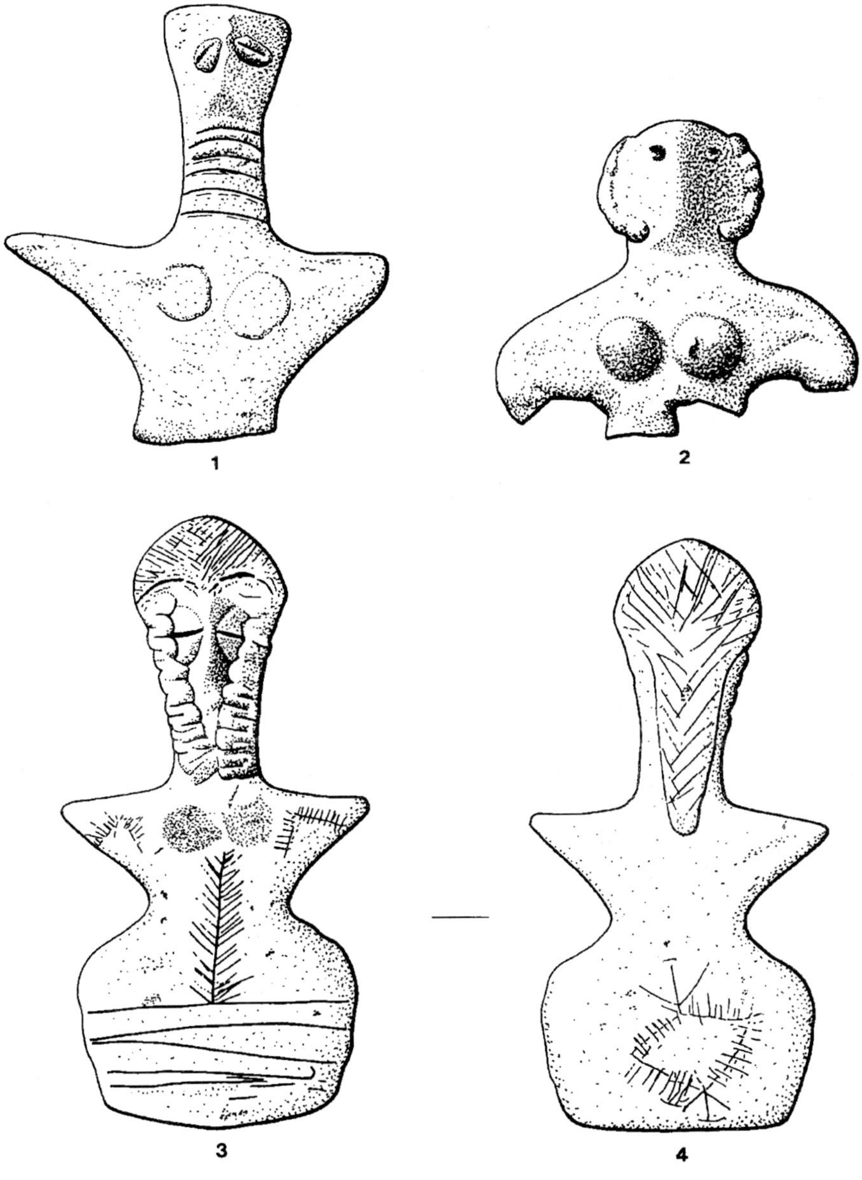

Fig. 13.

1. Turkmenia; 2. Namazga Tepe (After ADAMS *1968, Pl. 28.);*
3. Altyn Tepe (After MASSON *1968, Fig. 4. above).*

the Early Bronze Age connection between Egypt and Asia Minor should by no means be interpreted as reflecting the personal presence of Egyptians in Asia Minor, only as an indication of trade between the two regions.[123]

The overland caravan route existed already by the emergence of the Old Kingdom. The copper mines on the Sinai peninsula were probably worked by Semitic settlers from Arad, satisfying the demand for raw materials in Palestine, as shown by the pottery from scores of EB II settlements on the Sinai peninsula and also by the fact that when Arad was abandoned at the close of the EB II, life on these small mining settlements also ceased.[124]

Since the relics of Egyptian administration have not been found either at Arad, or at Tel Gath and En Basor, it seems unlikely that southern Palestine came under Egyptian rule either during the Old Kingdom or later. We should rather assume lively trade contacts.[125] These peaceful relations, a far cry from any form of military or administrative control, no doubt contributed to the flourishing of these towns during the Early Bronze Age.

The numerous alien population groups also brought changes to the cities of the eastern Mediterranean, the western Syrian littoral and the Levant. In the later phase of the Early Bronze Age there appeared a formerly unknown, good quality pottery ware – often considered by far the most beautiful Bronze Age pottery – in northern Palestine, in the settlements of the Jordan valley and Galilee. The distinctive red and black painted pottery, occasionally decorated with white relief patterns, was hand made, its surface was carefully smoothed and the orange slip was always polished. The ratio of this pottery ware within the ceramic inventory is so high as to preclude its interpretation as an import ware. This is also the southernmost distribution of this ware that only occurs sporadically south of Megiddo.[126] Arriving from the north, this ware became dominant also in northern Syria, one of the main centres of its distribution being the Plain of Antioch (today Antakya). Its homeland, however, should be sought even further afar, since its distribution can be traced through eastern Anatolia to southern Russia, to the Kura-Araxes Basin, where it may have ultimately originated.[127]

---

[123] HELCK 1979, p. 16.

[124] BEN-TOR 1981, p. 450.

[125] BEN-TOR 1981, p. 451.

[126] MELLAART 1966, p. 73.

[127] STAGER 1992, p. 39.

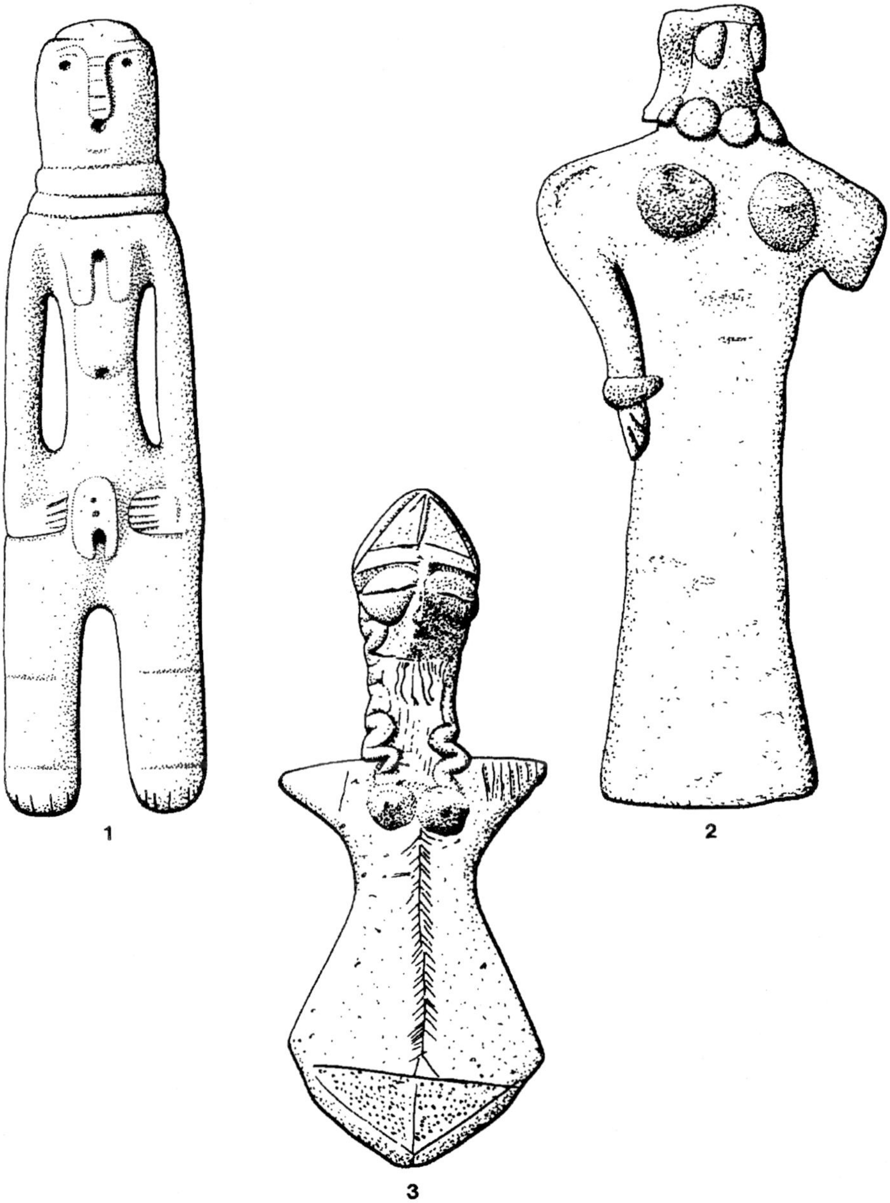

Fig. 14.

1. Tepe Yahya (After LAMBERG-KARLOVSKY *1986, Fig. 7.29);*
2. Braq (After MALLOWAN *1947, PL. 38/1);*
3. Altyn Tepe. (After MASSON *1968, Fig. 4. left below).*

Named after a site in Palestine, the Khirbet Kerak ware is homogenous to the extent that it was no doubt made by a specific population group. The ornamentation technique appears to have been a jealously guarded secret since it was never imitated.[128] At the same time, the fact that local wares continued to be made suggests that the presence of the Khirbet Kerak ware cannot be interpreted as an indication of invasion or destruction. The newcomers from the north apparently lived in peace with the local population.[129]

The map published by M. Roaf shows the extensive distribution of the Khirbet Kerak ware.[130] This distribution essentially corresponds to the middle and lower reaches of the Tigris and the Euphrates, i.e. the periphery encompassing the Mesopotamian core area from the west, the north and the east. This area includes, beside the Levant – the coastal strip of the Mediterranean – the upper reaches of the Euphrates and the Tigris, the region of Lake Van and Lake Urmia, as well as a part of the zone encompassing the Iranian plateau along the eastern slopes of the Zagros Mountains. This pottery style borders on the two major 3rd millennium pottery wares, the Niniveh 5 and the Diyala region pottery in the north and the east. Roaf has suggested that the Khirbet Kerak ware can be traced to an early Transcaucasian pottery style that was distributed south of the Caucasus.[131] A new, previously unknown architecture also appears on the sites with Khirbet Kerak ware. Larger and more carefully constructed multi-roomed houses were erected within the fortified settlements. The rooms were roofed with domes, resembling the rural architecture of present-day Arab villages. The eponymous site yielded the earliest carbonized olive kernel seeds known to date, as well as idols and pot sherds with bull's heads in relief.[132]

The distinctive, common finds of the Mesopotamian periphery can thus be seen to comprise not only idols. A fortified settlement with round houses resembling the EB III settlement at Khirbet Kerak was uncovered at Yanik Tepe near Lake Urmia. Large-scale excavation activity during the past decades has yielded further evidence for a flourishing trade in the later 3rd millennium.

---

[128] Mellaart 1966, p. 73.

[129] Mellaart 1966, p. 74.

[130] Roaf 1998, p. 80.

[131] Roaf 1998, p. 80.

[132] Mellaart 1966, p. 76.

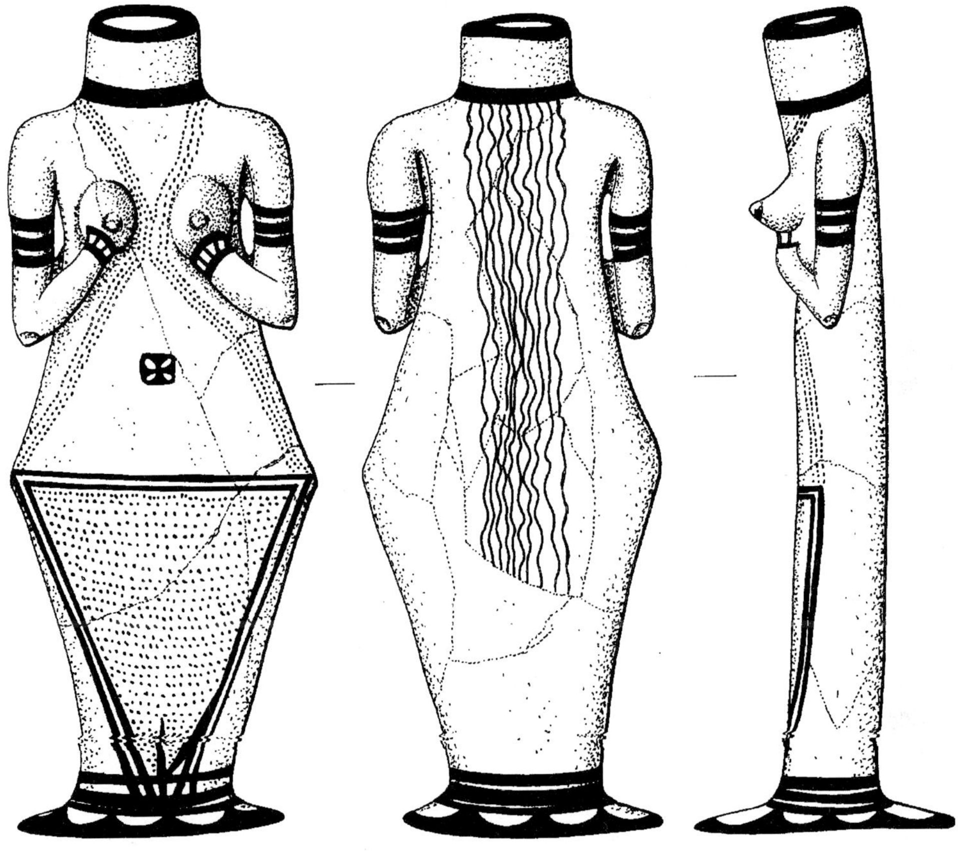

Fig. 15.

Yarim Tepe (After MERPERT – MUNČAEV *1981, Fig. 98).*

The finds from Tepe Yahya, Tal-i-Iblis, Shahdad, Shahr-i-Sokhta, Mundigak and Bampur reveal that lapis lazuli and other precious stones (primarily chlorite, a soft greenish stone) and various items made from them, as well as stone axes, metal artefacts, tin, beads and female idols were traded from the Baluchistan Mountains and Iran.[133] These metal artefacts and idols also reached the settlements of the early Indus valley civilization from Tepe Yahya, suggesting that this site, together with Tepe Siyalk, Tepe Giyan and the late 3rd millennium settlement at Tell Ašmar had been trading centres mediating between east and west.[134] According to Chr. Burney various eastern population groups had settled at Tell Ašmar,[135] and that similarly to Byblos and the majority of the towns in southern Palestine, the Egyptians also controlled this major strategic point of the eastern trade route. M. Tosi reached a similar conclusion based on his excavations at Shahr-i-Sokhta, lying on the border between Iran and Afghanistan.[136]

Idols thus reached faraway regions in the cultural province that was both characterized and moulded by this early, trans-Caucasian flourishing trade. According to M. Tosi's statistics the number of these figurines increased – parallel to the growth of the Shahr-i-Sokhta settlement – in the later 3rd millennium, but virtually disappeared by the time of the Third Dynasty of Ur and the rise of Elam.[137] The Soviet and Russian investigations in southern Turkmenia have yielded a wealth of new information on the settlements lying on the fringes of the Caspian littoral, the mountainous region and the Iranian desert, as well as on the trade routes linking them.[138] As mentioned in the section discussing the typology of the Budapest idol (see pp. 13), the figurines from Djejtun, Namazga Tepe and Altin Tepe, although different, nonetheless

---

[133] Kohl 1978, p. 24; Burney 1975, p. 192; Lamberg – Karlovsky 1972, pp. 222–229; Stager 1992, p. 39. The evidence for trade in tin is more uncertain: it is only mentioned on the clay tablets from Kültepe, dated to the 2nd millennium. It has nonetheless been suggested that tin, necessary for bronzeworking, had been imported into northern Mesopotamia and southeast Anatolia from Afghanistan via the Iranian plateau as early as the 3rd millennium. Cf. Roaf 1998, p. 113.

[134] Burney 1977, p. 55.

[135] Burney 1975, p. 195.

[136] Tosi 1973, pp. 424–446; Tosi 1978, pp. 57–77.

[137] Tosi 1978, p. 70.

[138] Masson 1968, pp. 178–187; Masson – Korobkova 1989, pp. 62–70; Masson 1978.

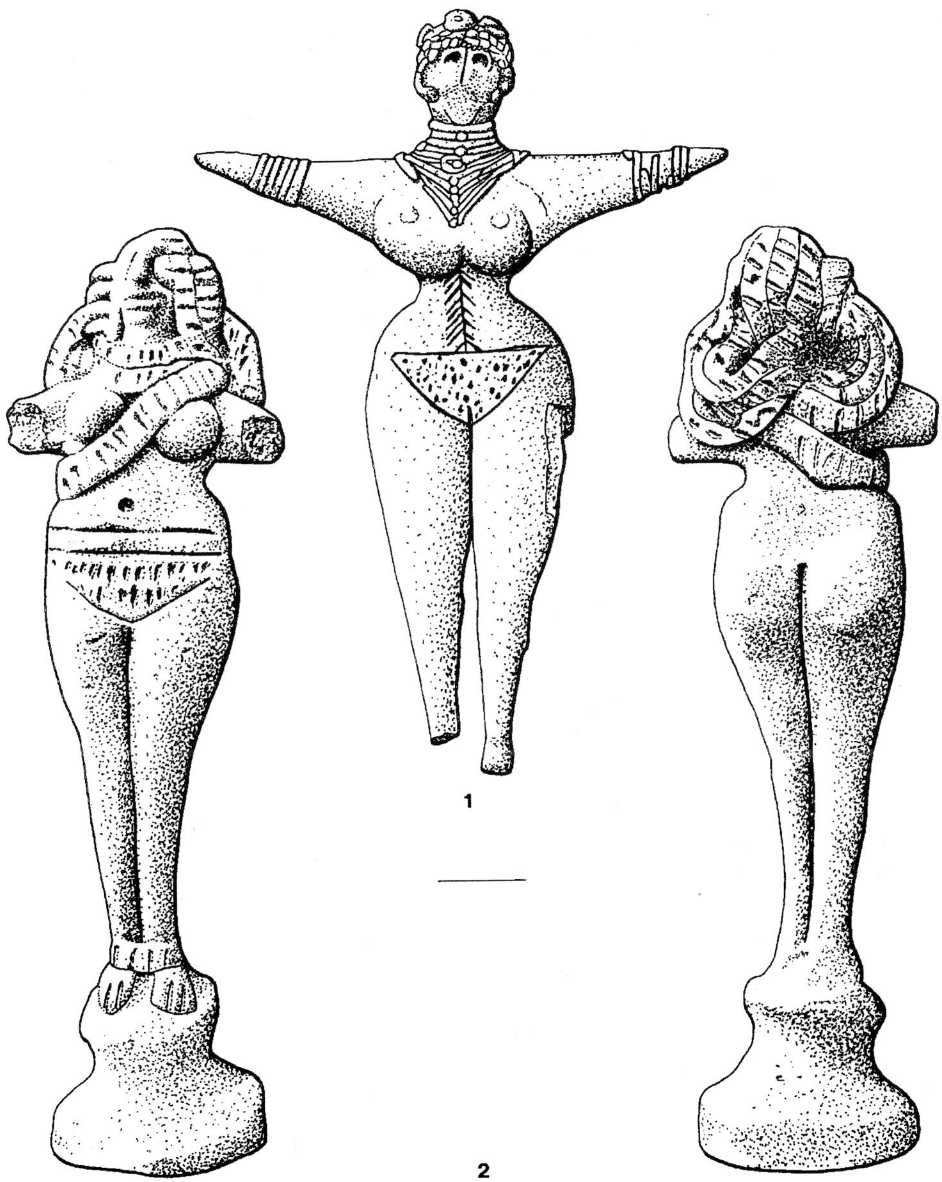

Fig. 16.

1. Turang Tepe (After PORADA *1962, Fig. 16.);*
2. Susa (After AMIET *1977, Fig. 418, 419).*

reflect a certain typological (and, most likely, spiritual) relation with the figurines from Syro-Palestine and Iran, as well as with the Afghanistan ones, as shown by the Bronze Age finds from the sites along the route skirting the Iranian plateau from the north published by V. M. Masson and V. I. Sarianidi,[139] and the figurines from Tepe Hissar,[140] as well as the idols found at Susa and Tepe Yahya, settlements lying on the southern route.[141] The eastern destination of both the northern route, leading through Mundigak and the other mountain settlements, and the southern route, passing through Tepe Yahya, Kulli, Damb Sadaat, Quetta and the Zhob valley, was the early Indus valley civilization.[142] There no doubt evolved a *koine* along these trade routes that encompassed not only the various trade commodities and utilitarian artefacts, but also the lifeways of the affected population groups.[143]

The luxury and prestige commodities traded along the Mediterranean coast, the eastern Iranian and the Afghanistan trade routes during the 3rd millennium included also female figurines modelled from clay. The juxtaposing of the known and published finds, complemented with new typological observations, offers a plausible explanation for the numerous similarities between the idols of such an extensive area.

The commodities listed in the above – all from find assemblages uncovered and analyzed at greater length during the past decades – which attest the existence of a flourishing long-distance trade in the 3rd millennium form a well-circumscribed assemblage which scholars have labelled Intercultural Style.[144] This label is based on the typological and chemical analysis of chlorite vessels, as well as on clay vessels and various items made from precious stones, and, we may most certainly add, terracotta figurines – namely the idols. This hypothesis is confirmed by the few chlorite figurines from Tepe Yahya, clothed in the woollen kilt, the *kaunakes* of Sumer. Beside providing an explanation of what the Mesopotamians gave in exchange for these luxury goods, this also suggests that the Intercultural Style "demonstrates

---

139 Masson – Sarianidi 1973.

140 Schmidt 1937, Pls 27 B and 45.

141 Spycket 1992.

142 Gajjar 1971.

143 Schlossmann 1975, p. 332.

144 Kohl 1978, p. 23.

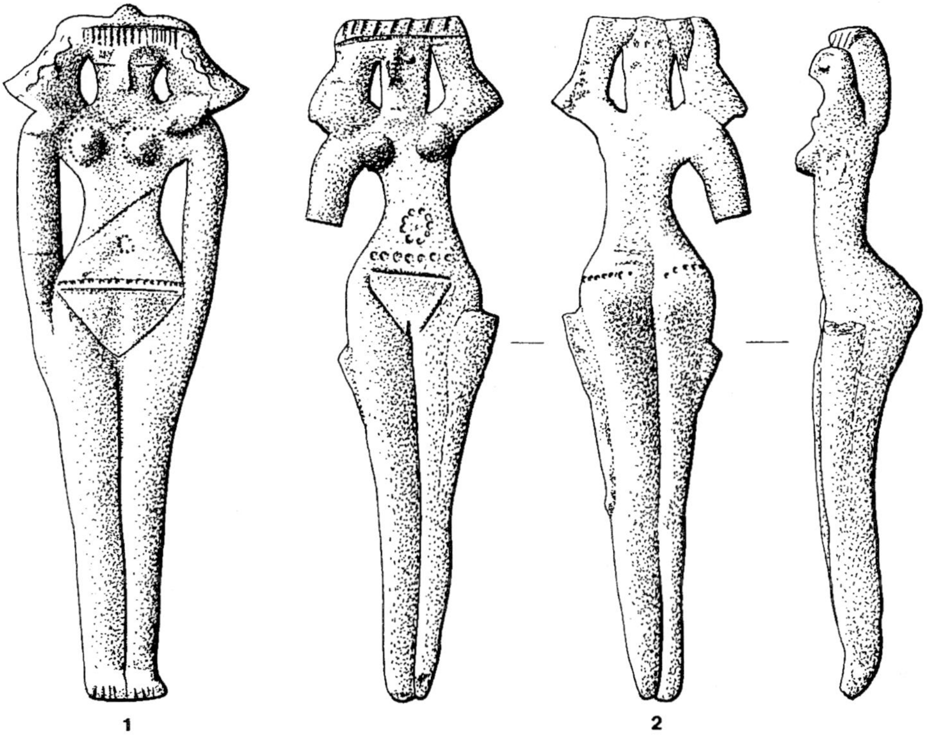

Fig. 17.

1. Syria (After Bossert 1951, Fig. 631);
2. Egypt (After Morenz 1975, Figs. 19, 20).

a recognition of complex symbols or an iconographic tradition over a vast, culturally heterogeneous area."[145] Symbols, and their representations, obviously also spread in the opposite direction: the figure of the bearded bull, a well-known type in Sumerian art, can probably be traced to the bull cult flourishing in the Namazga V period which, for example, can be demonstrated at Altin Tepe at the close of the 3rd millennium.[146]

However, we must by necessity also assume the movement of individuals, merchants and, also, population groups behind the various commodities reaching distant areas through long-distance trade.

Signs that less peaceful tribes than the population manufacturing the Khirbet Kerak ware had appeared in the Levant, where Egyptian officials kept a strong control on both ends of the marine trade route, can be noted at the end of the Old Kingdom. The unrest began under Pepi I's rule. The inscription on the tomb of one of his officials who died around 2300 BC mentions punitive raids on the rebellious tribes in southern Palestine which may have reached Mount Carmel.[147] Shortly after Byblos VI was burnt, trade ceased with the coastal towns, while Asian hordes invaded the Nile Delta. The destruction of Byblos can probably also be related to these invasions. Jericho was also torched and invaded, similarly to a number of other Syro-Palestinian towns of the EB III in the 21st century.[148] A contemporary destruction layer can also be noted in the Early Bronze Age towns of southern Anatolia.[149]

The nomadic incursions into Egypt were in part made possible by the weakening of local power. In the last period of the Old Kingdom the merchants increased the power of both the pharaohs and the *nomoi*, which began to fight with each other.[150] As a result of these local bids for independence, petty 'kings' came into power in Lower Egypt, in the south and, later, also in the north: "seventy kings ruled for seventy days". The breakdown of the

---

[145] KOHL 1978, p. 28.

[146] TOSI 1978, pp. 57–77, here p. 62. Tosi also notes the similarities in iconography between the artwork of distant regions.

[147] MELLAART 1966, p. 70.

[148] MELLAART 1979, pp. 6–18, and the chronological chart on p. 18; MELLAART 1966, pp. 91–92.

[149] YAKAR 1976, pp. 156–157.

[150] JIDEJIAN 1971, p. 21; DAUMAS 1969, pp. 89–91.

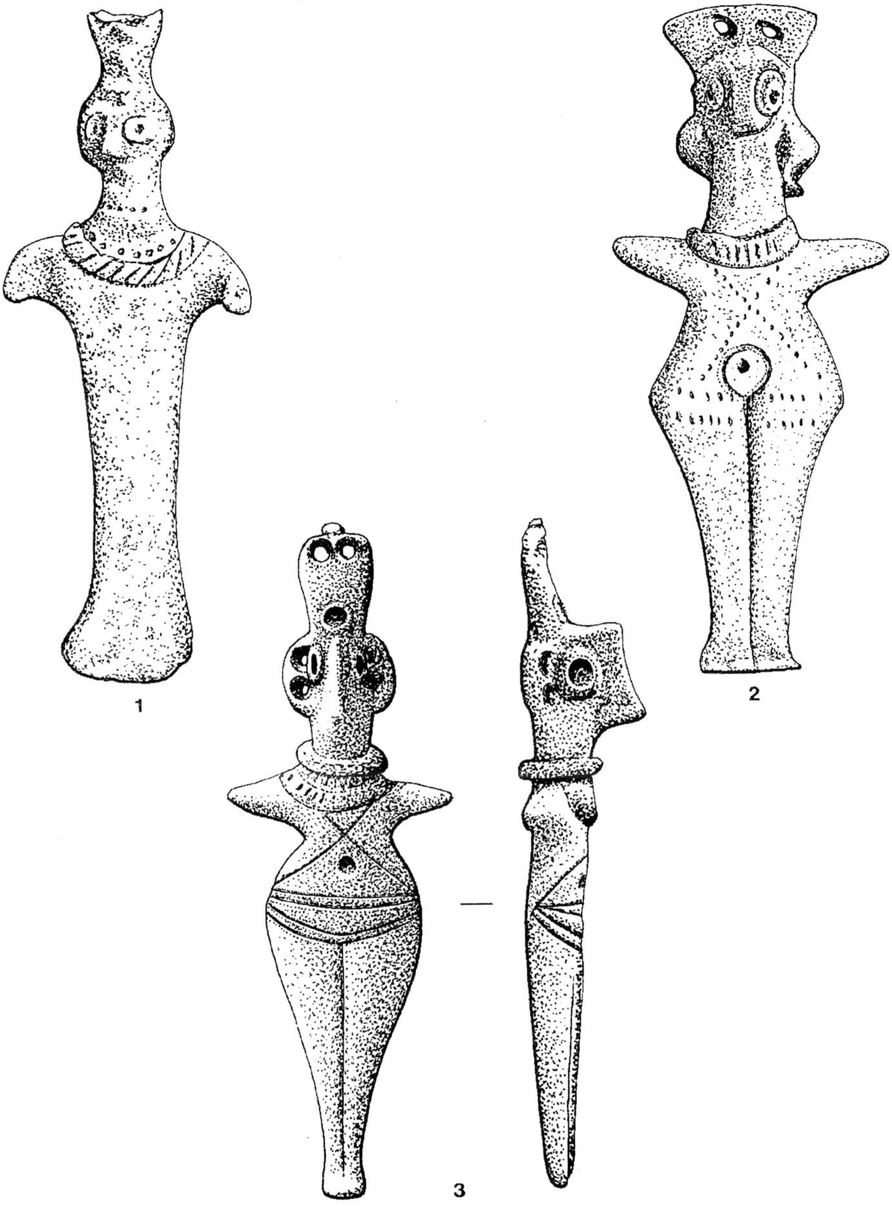

Fig. 18.

1. Northern Syria (After DANNHEIMER *1985, p. 93, Cat. Nr. 38a);*
2. Hama (After BOSSERT *1951, p. 193, Fig. 630);*
3. Syria (After BOSSERT *1951, p. 193, Fig. 628).*

centralized administration led to a decline in food production, and the famine in its wake caused population migrations, rebellions fuelled by widespread famine and smaller local conflicts. The Nile Delta came under the control of Bedouin tribes.[151]

A similar turmoil and unrest characterized the Syro-Palestinian settlements at the close of the Early Bronze Age. The Khirbet Kerak settlements in northern Palestine also perished, some overlain with a layer containing local wares.[152] In Byblos trade ceased after the reign of Pepi II (VIth Dynasty) and a new nomadic people, arriving from Anatolia, appeared over the entire Near East. Only Kheti III of the Xth Dynasty, ruling in the First Intermediate Period, managed to drive these nomads from the Nile Delta, and trade resumed with the Byblos.[153] After a long hiatus, the first Egyptian inscription from Byblos, recording the revival of trade in cedar between Egypt and Lebanon, dates from the XIth Dynasty. Trade between Byblos and southern Mesopotamia is evidenced by a clay tablet dating from the time of the Third Dynasty of Ur that mentions the name of this coastal merchant town.[154] At the turn of the 3rd and 2nd millennium, all major settlements in Canaan were occupied by nomadic tribes who adopted a sedentary way of life, their social structure determined by the urban organization. Their relative newness to sedentism is also attested by the poorer quality of their architecture. The earlier fine Khirbet Kerak ware was replaced by a less than pleasing, uniform pottery. Their metallurgy, however, was excellent.[155]

Who were these nomads? And what other features did they share beside their Mid-Eastern origins and their nomadic lifeways? What language did they speak, to which language family did they belong? One important component of these groups is that they undoubtedly spoke a Semitic language, as evidenced by the Execration Texts of the XIIth Dynasty, magical spells expressing curses on all enemies, both real and potential, inscribed on pottery that was then ritually smashed.[156] Some of the tribes which had settled on

---

[151] Kákosy 1998, 107–111, with extensive quotes from the Admonitions of Ipuwer, one of the best sources on the turmoil and unrest during the First Intermediate Period.

[152] Mellaart 1966, p. 91.

[153] Mellaart 1966, p. 71.

[154] Jidejian 1971, pp. 22–23.

[155] Mellaart 1966, pp. 93–94.

[156] Roaf 1998, p. 118.

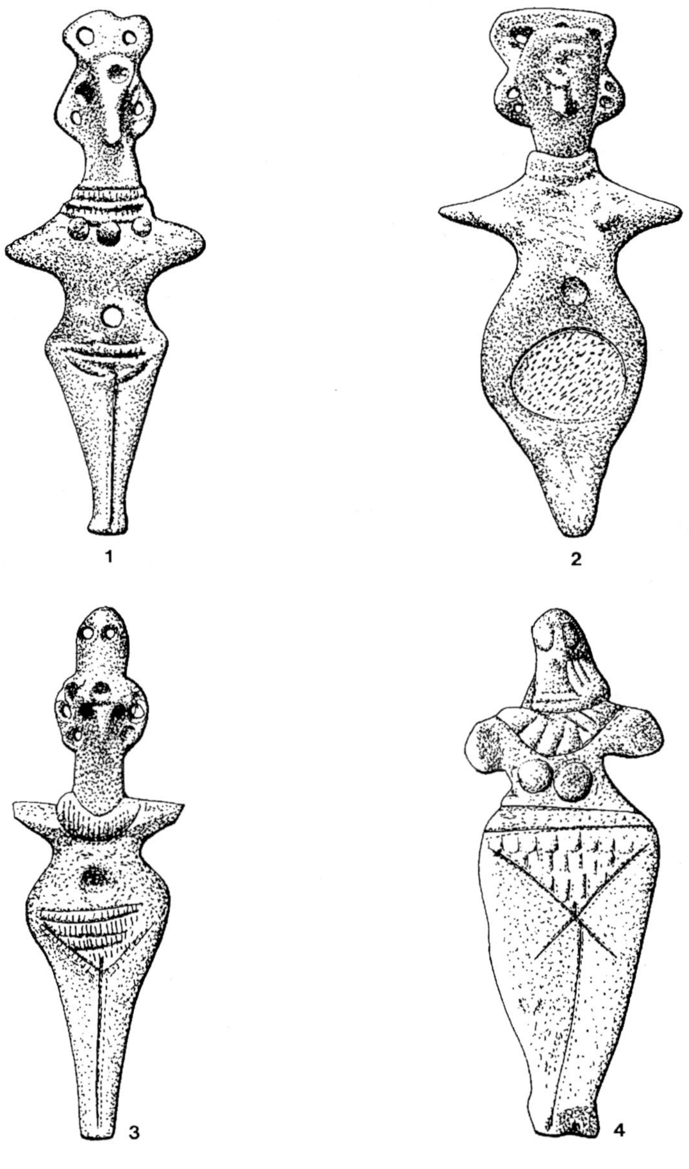

Fig. 19.

1. Northern Syria (After Dannheimer *1985, p. 93, Cat. Nr. 44 left);*
2. Sam'al (After Klengel *1977, Fig. 4);*
3. Sam'al (After Klengel *1977, Fig. 5);*
4. Isin (After Hrouda *1975, Fig. 4).*

the coast were later known as Canaanites, while the inland tribes were called Amorites,[157] although the name Canaanite is sometimes applied to all those Semitic tribes which had controlled Syro-Palestine from the Early Bronze Age to the Iron Age.[158] However, even relatively small regions were not uniform as shown by the customs that have survived in the archaeological record. In Jericho, for example, at least two groups can be distinguished on the basis of the funerary rites: one group buried its men with daggers, the other laid vessels into the grave. At Tell el-Ajjul the presence of several groups, each with its own burial customs, was observed.[159]

Beside Semitic tribes, there undoubtedly lived several other nomadic peoples on the fringes of Mesopotamia. Some of these tribes are mentioned in the cuneiform texts from Mesopotamia and in Sumerian poetry,[160] while others disappeared without a trace. The Guti or Qutu group from the Zagros Mountains must here be mentioned, which at the close of the 3rd millennium invaded Mesopotamia and swept away the remnants of the empire of Sargon of Akkad.[161] Another group, arriving from a more northerly and easterly region, must also be mentioned in this respect, namely the Hurrians, who stand unrelated to any Semitic or Indo-European speaking population group,[162] and who are often identified with the main bearers of the early trans-Caucasian culture,[163] while their early groups (called proto-Hurrians or a group speaking a Hurri dialect) are very often equated with the makers of the Khirbet Kerak ware.[164] This may have been the first wave of the nomadic peoples' migration from the northeast to the Levant.[165] Their first tangible traces can be dated to the mid-3rd millennium, and they gradually moved to the coastal areas in southern Syria.[166] Their original homeland probably lay east of the Tigris.

---

157 MELLAART 1966, p. 93.

158 BEN-TOR 1981, pp. 449–451.

159 MELLAART 1966, pp. 93–94.

160 KOMORÓCZY 1978, pp. 87–96.

161 L. OPPENHEIM 1964, pp. 402–403.

162 HAAG (ed.) 1981, p. 763.

163 ROAF 1998, p. 108.

164 DJAKONOV 1981, pp. 88–89.

165 MORENZ 1975, p. 45.

166 GELB 1944, p. 89.

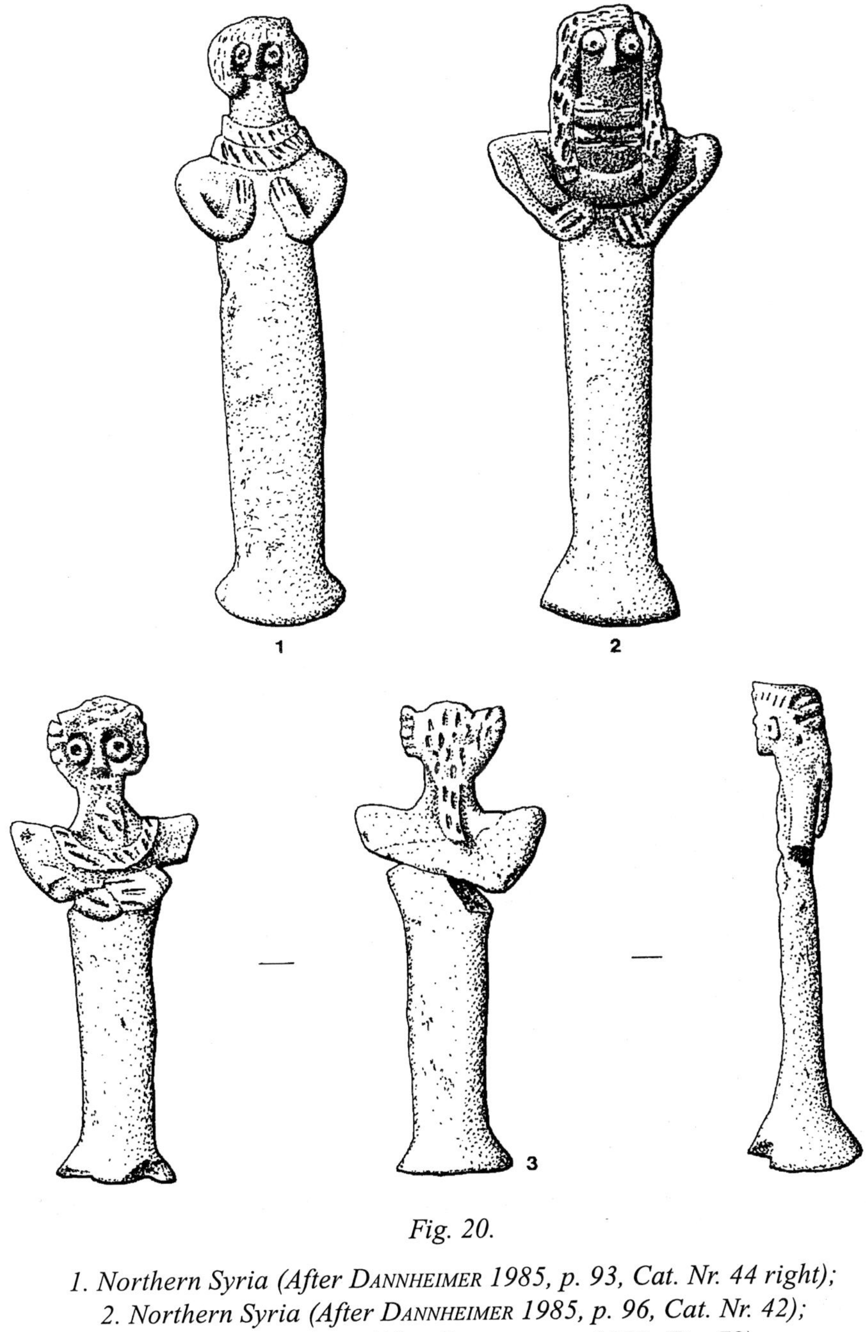

Fig. 20.

1. Northern Syria (After DANNHEIMER *1985, p. 93, Cat. Nr. 44 right);*
2. Northern Syria (After DANNHEIMER *1985, p. 96, Cat. Nr. 42);*
3. Habuba Kabira (After STROMMENGER *1980, Fig. 78).*

The Sargonid rulers led several campaigns against the Hurrians who had settled north of the Orontes and along the Khabur. Mellaart has noted that the series of circular fortified towns, most probably occupied by Hurrians, appear to have formed a fortified boundary. These towns include Tell Huwera on the present-day Syrian-Turkish border whose counter-fort can be identified with Naram Sin's palace at Brak.[167] This military spirit can hardly have been the norm on the periphery since Hurrian merchants played an important role from the Levant through Anatolia to the Iranian plateau. Over one-half of the names in the texts uncovered at Alalah, a town lying on the Orontes in western Syria, are Hurrian.[168] Based on his excavation of the Bronze Age layers of the Lidar Höyük tell settlement on the middle Euphrates, H. Hauptmann considers this Early Bronze Age settlement to have been Hurrian.[169] Roaf has also suggested that Hurrian gods had been adopted over extensive areas, including Anatolian population groups.[170] It must here also be noted that Helck categorically attributes the late 3rd millennium Syro-Palestinian idol type – to which the Budapest figurine can also be assigned – to the Hurrians.[171] G. F. Dales has noted that the "evidence proves beyond any doubt that the typical North Syrian figurines in question followed chronologically their Mesopotamian prototypes. Significantly, the appearance of the North Syrian figurines coincides exactly with growing powers and influence of the Hurrians in that area. It has been suggested that the North Syrian figurines are a Hurri adaptation of Mesopotamian Ur III and Isin-Larsa images. ... Probably this reflects the Hurrian penetration into Palestine attested to by other groups of evidence."[172]

In the later 3rd millennium there evolved a cultural and trade *koine* on the western, northern and eastern periphery of Mesopotamia, no doubt with the active participation of the Hurrian tribes, which naturally reflects the influence of the Mesopotamian civilization, but is at the same time characteristically

---

[167] Mellaart 1966, p. 92.

[168] Roaf 1998, p. 108.

[169] Hauptmann 1993, p. 12.

[170] Roaf 1998, p. 108. Burney suggested that the Hittites, arriving from the Caucasus, found a Hurrian aboriginal population in eastern Anatolia. Burney – Lang 1971, pp. 88–89.

[171] W. Helck quotes A. Moortgat when mentioning the unprovenanced idols housed in Bremen. Helck 1971, p. 48.

[172] Dales 1960, p. 247.

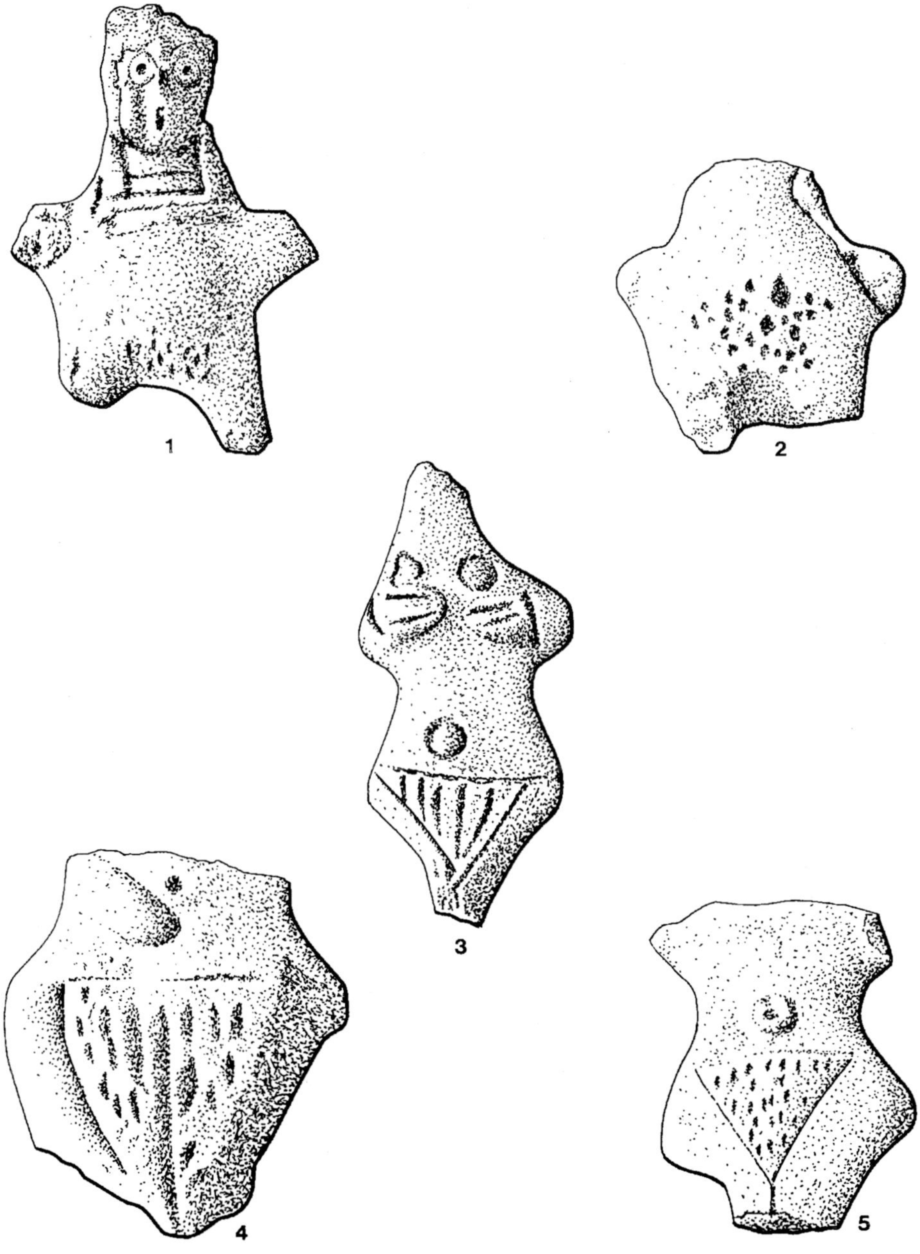

Fig. 21.

1–5. Tell Taya (After Reade 1973).

peripheral and shows an interaction over an extensive area, from the Nile Delta through the Syrian littoral to the mountain regions of the Euphrates, the Khabur and the Tigris, and extending to even more easterly territories, to southern Turkmenia and the Makran region south of the Iranian desert. Its importance has been repeatedly emphasized by M. Tosi,[173] and has been most succinctly expressed by L. Oppenheim: "A civilization of the magnitude and duration of the Mesopotamian cannot but exercise a radiation pressure which only formidable geographical barriers are able to screen off. We must therefore assume a halo-like peripheral zone about the satellite civilizations, a zone into which a number of Mesopotamian objects, ideas and practices slowly infiltrated or were brought as spoils by booty-laden mountaineers returning from razzias into Mesopotamian territory, carried by traders or remained after the short-lived attempts of Babylonia and Assyria to create buffer-states by colonizing the unruly tribesmen. Mesopotamian influence, in varying degrees of intensity, must have spread and been diffused along routes much further into and beyond the Iranian plateau, Afghanistan, and the littoral of the Caspian Sea and that of the Aegean than we have any well-documented reason to believe."[174]

The population movements on the periphery of Mesopotamia, the fine pottery wares that can be associated with these migrations, the association with the Hurrians – as illustrated by the maps published by M. Roaf – shows a remarkable correspondence with the distribution of another find type, namely the figurines resembling the Budapest idol. This would suggest that the distribution of the standing, bejewelled figurines with applied eyes, that had evolved from the Neolithic traditions of northern Mesopotamia and Anatolia, cannot be dissociated from the makers of the Khirbet Kerak ware, a population group that is often labelled proto-Hurrian.

As we have seen, this population cannot be assigned to either the early Indo-European, or the Semitic language family. The same conclusion was reached concerning the bearers of the early Indus valley civilization. Their language has still not been deciphered, even though there is an abundant corpus of inscribed seals.[175] Still, the general consensus is that the Indus valley

---

[173] Tosi 1978, p. 61.

[174] L. Oppenheim 1964, pp. 71–72.

[175] Burrow 1969, 274–278.

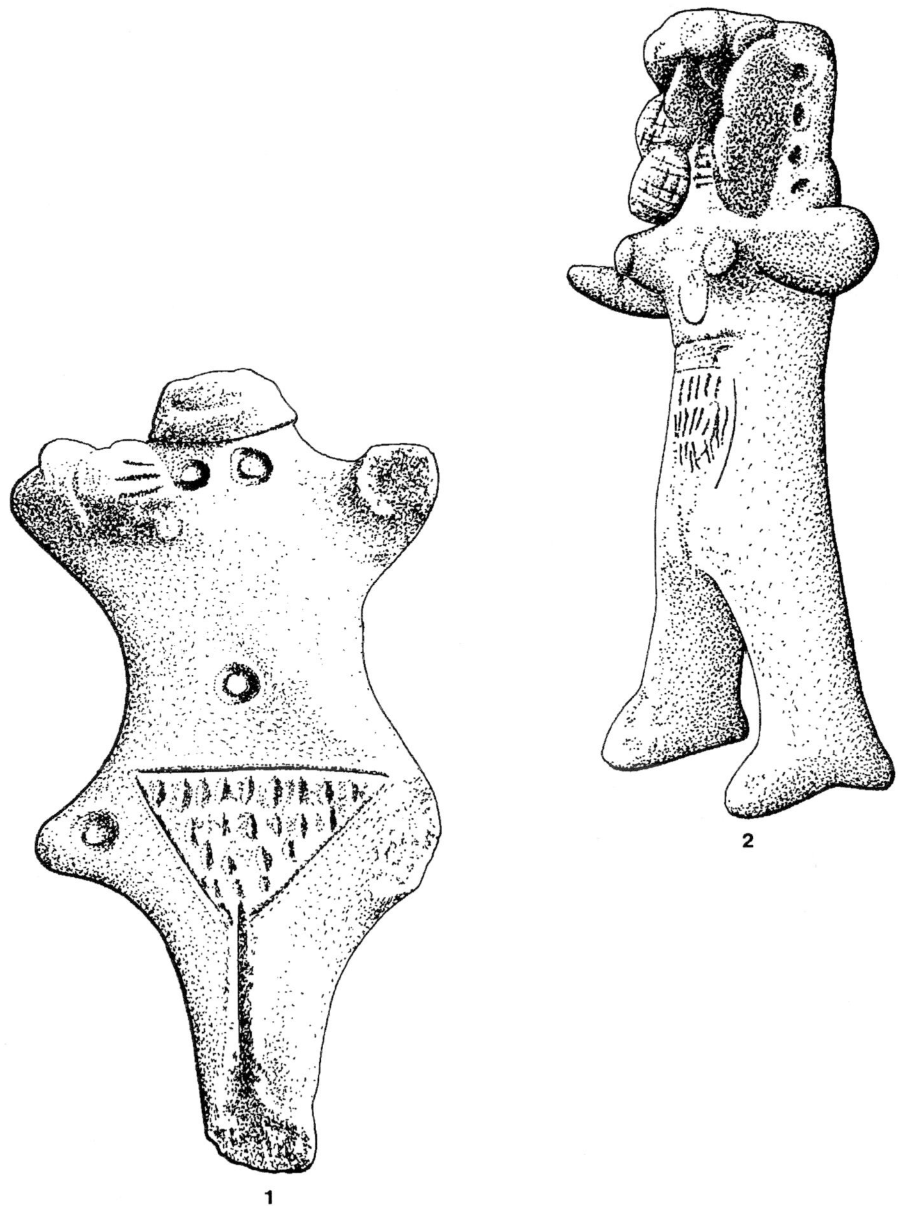

Fig. 22.

1. Tell Taya (After R*EADE 1973);*
2. Babylonia (After A*MIET 1977, Fig. 429).*

civilization can most likely be identified with the ancestors of the Dravidians who had been driven to southern India by the Aryans. Obviously, the proto-Hurrian and the proto-Dravidian populations cannot be associated with each other simply because they both spoke an unknown tongue and because so little is known about them. Scholars researching the emergence of the Indus valley civilization tend to attach greater importance to the mediation of the merchants arriving from the northern and southern side of the Iranian plateau than to a genuine immigration to the Baluchi Mountains. As a matter of fact, it is exactly these trade relations that make the mediation of cultural influences most likely since there is evidence for the exchange of raw material such as lapis lazuli and various artefacts made from chlorite between the west and the Afghanistan highland, and the pottery from the earliest settlements of Indus valley civilizations – Kulli and Mehi – has a distinctly Iranian flavour.

The striking similarities in human figurines can also be assigned here. Beside the merchants, we may also assume other, hitherto unknown non-Indo-European and non-Semitic mountain nomad tribes as mediating cultural influences. That these tribes doubtless existed is evidenced by the Mesopotamian and Egyptian written sources, as well as by certain references to 2nd millennium history that have been preserved in the Old Testament.

There appear the contours of a historical background in which the formerly unimaginable may be envisioned, namely the occurrence of an Early Bronze artefact type is areas lying far away from each other. This artefact type, then, was distributed from Egypt to Afghanistan through the Beqaa valley and the Orontes region along an overland route or to Antiochia on the marine route, to the Zagros Mountains in western Iran, to Lake Van and Lake Urmia, and, skirting the Iranian plateau, to Baluchistan.

It must be emphasized that the Budapest idol and the similar figurines cannot be regarded as artefacts made and used by nomads – they are the relics of a settled, agrarian population. Their distribution over such an extensive area, however, cannot be conceived without long-distance trade and the caravans of the Hurrians and other nomadic tribes whose names have not been preserved.

Up to this point, we have spoken of these figurines as one of the many commodities that had been traded, as if there were no difference between a jug for storing olive oil and a clay idol.

One problem of prehistory may have been solved and – similarly to the results of the typological analysis – this has raised another, more difficult issue

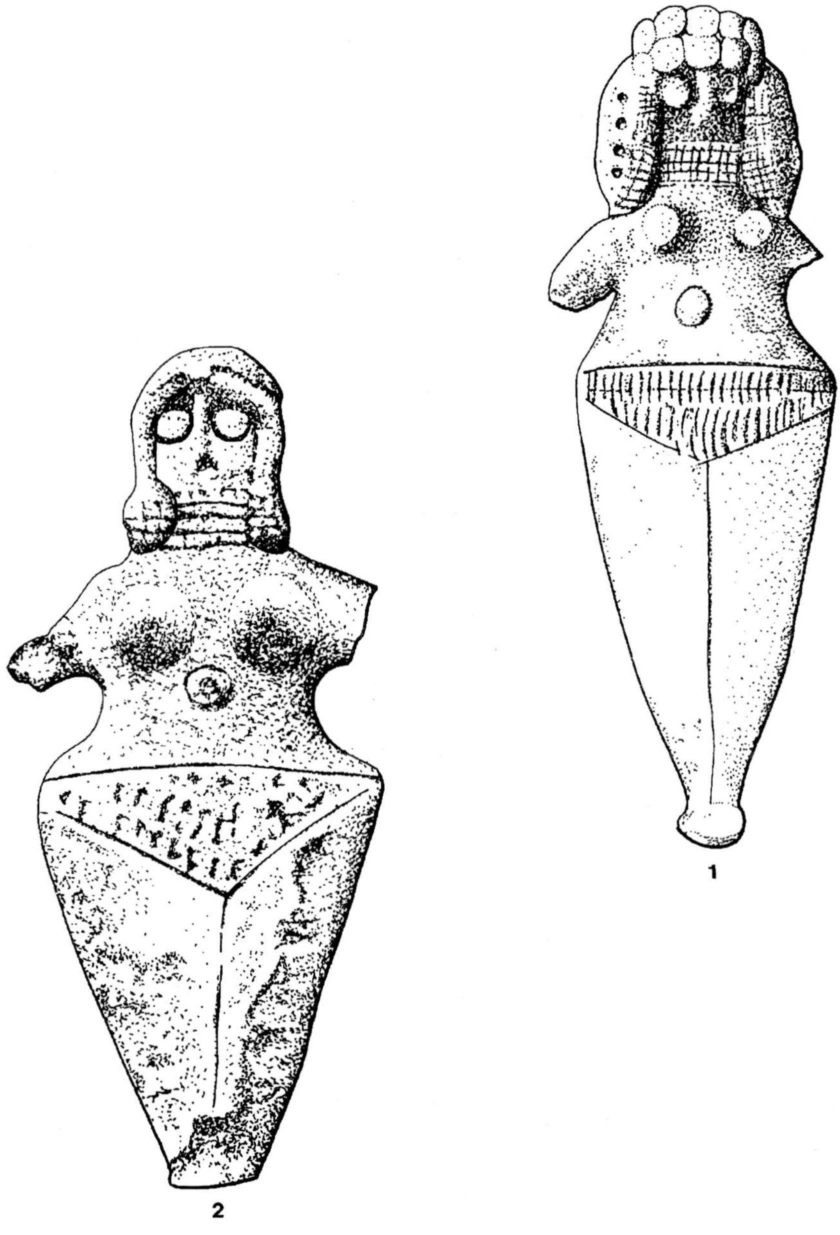

Fig. 23.

1. Tell Asmar (After Müller*-*Karpe *1974, Fig. 206/24);*
2. Mesopotamia (After Amiet *1977, Fig. 430).*

since this is not an artefact of day to day use, stone or metal raw material, or luxury item, such as olive oil, but rather a statuette which can be interpreted in a sacral, rather than a profane context, and which is distinguished from the artefacts of day to day use in that it only held a meaning in the community in which it had been made. Therefore we can hardly break off the discussion of the Budapest idol without attempting to describe and reconstruct the religious background, the ritual and the social context which enabled figurines such as the Budapest idol to be vested with a meaning in communities which lay scattered over a vast area.

The religious background

There is perhaps no other prehistoric artefact type which has been analyzed so often and so diversely as idols, and one which has fallen prey to the most controversial interpretations. Since the commencement of regular excavations in the Near East and South-East Europe, these finds were usually divorced from the other, 'less interesting' finds with which they were found and published 'out of context'. In this 'decontextualized' form, idols could at the most be analyzed stylistically or within the framework of art history, while the possible context for their function vanished into thin air and only educated guesses were proposed.[176] Many such guesses were made. The most common pitfall to these interpretations was that most analyses were based on the external features of these idols and most interpretations were unable to break free of modern patterns of thought. For example, each and every emphatically female figurine was usually associated with the concept of fertility. This, in fact, is what we today believe, in other words, it is the projection of our own cultural concepts back into an age that did not necessarily think along the same lines. As will be clear from the following, the association of figurines depicting females with fertility and motherhood are mostly invalid for the prehistoric idols of the Near East.

One result of projecting our own ideas back into the past as an analytical approach is that in many publications discussing idols, the description of the idol and its assignment to an archaeological culture and period is followed by a few commonplaces of interpretation: the idol either depicts the Great Goddess, the Magna Mater, and it was used in fertility and agrarian rites. Even though each word of the latter sentence would deserve a separate analysis, these commonplaces have hardened into a veritable Neolithic religion. M. Gimbutas must certainly be mentioned here, for her many studies in this field, if nothing else.[177] Based on the theories on evolutionism and matriarchy of the 19th century, she proceeded to create a Neolithic golden age filled with a pantheon of goddesses, which was sadly destroyed – once and for all – by the incursion of patriarchal Indo-European tribes at the dawn of the Early Bronze

---

[176] For an overview cf. Bánffy 1986b, pp. 152–157; Goodison – Morris 1998, pp. 6–21.

[177] Gimbutas 1982; Gimbutas 1989a, Chapter 7; Gimbutas 1989b; Gimbutas 1991.

Age. Her views, based on "argumentation by assertion",[178] are little more than fanciful conjectures. Still, Gimbutas cannot be blamed for weaving political strands into the tapestry of the golden age of matriarchy. The feminists of the west coast in the United States incorporated Gimbutas' ideas into the ideology of their political struggle.[179] This direction, coupled with the earlier psychologizing approach based on Jung's theories,[180] resulted in that the advocates of the New Archaeology dismissed whole-heartedly not only the attempts at interpretation, but also any research in this field. Any study of idols in the heyday of scientific methods in archaeology became a contemptible pastime.

This view too proved to be a dead end. Idols and the entire corpus of other cultic finds were a far too important source, especially in prehistoric periods which had no written records, to be excluded from analysis simply owing to a few ill-starred attempts. Aside from a few fanciful and absurd ideas,[181] and a more recent study lamenting the end of the New Archaeology,[182] the analysis of idols has perhaps now found its proper place in prehistoric research. The careful documentation and evaluation of the archaeological context will provide a way out from this impasse.

The best approach still seems to be a 'loving description',[183] followed by a thorough typological analysis and a description of possible find associations. One possibility for orphaned idols, divorced from their find context, is the reconstruction of the historical, social and, possibly, religious background: the ages and functions which can be rejected, and the ones into which it can be plausibly fitted. This study is concerned with an idol whose find circumstances and contexts are wholly unknown and thus the next, perhaps

---

[178] Gimbutas' arguments have recently been criticized by M. Conkey and R. Tringham. CONKEY – TRINGHAM 1995, pp. 199–247, and esp. p. 216.

[179] One good example is M. Stone's *When God was a woman*. STONE 1976.

[180] Its best-known representative was perhaps E. Neumann. NEUMANN 1956.

[181] According to D. Bailey, the multitude of female idols made by women was a backlash against the patriarchic rule; the figurines supposedly depict individuals, namely their makers. This analysis was based on Bulgarian finds. BAILEY 1996, pp. 291–295.

[182] UCKO 1996, pp. 300–304.

[183] This expression is quoted by L. Goodison and Chr. Morris from Susan Sontag. Goodison – MORRIS 1998, p. 15.

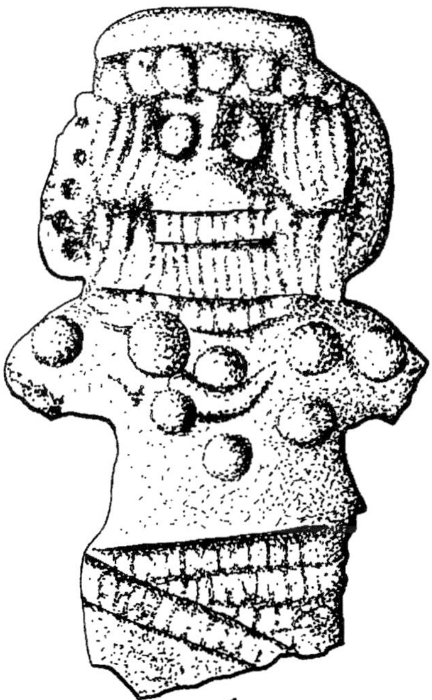

1

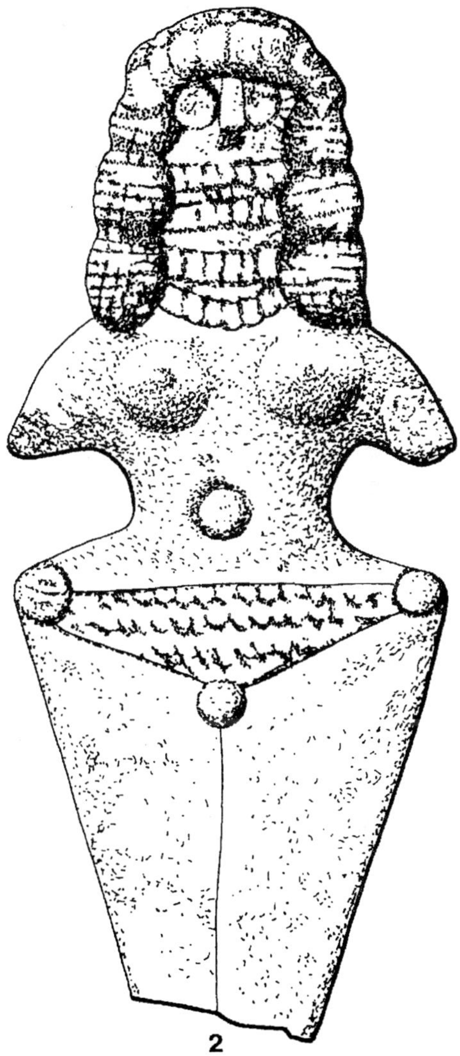

2

Fig. 24.

1. Tell Asmar (After MÜLLER-KARPE *1974, Fig. 206/22);*
2. Tell Asmar (After MÜLLER-KARPE *1974, Fig. 206/26).*

most important phase which determines the boundaries of interpretation, i.e. the analysis of the archaeological context,[184] is not possible.

The only course open to further analysis is a discussion of the probability of the three most likely find contexts. Idols had either been placed in a burial, they may come from a sanctuary or from a settlement context: a house, a special area within a house set aside for domestic cults, from a pit beside a house, which may have been a sacrificial pit, a foundation trench or a simply a refuse pit.

(1) Idols from burials

If an idol is intact or almost completely intact, there is a distinct possibility that it comes from a grave since settlement finds tend to be broken. One interesting phenomenon – still unexplained – is that with the exception of a few cultures, such as the Hamangia culture of the Lower Danube area or the Early Bronze Age burials in the Cyclades, idols had not been deposited in burials during the Neolithic in Central and South-East Europe.

A number of idols are known from the burials of the Ubaid culture, flourishing in the 5th millennium BC in the Near East. The two hundred graves of the cemetery uncovered at Eridu yielded several idols,[185] most of which had lain beside the hips or placed in the hands of the deceased.[186] V. M. Masson has published idols found in graves from southern Turkmenia.[187] A. Jirku mentions the burial chamber in Megiddo dated to 2100 BC and the 15–20 cm high, 2–3 cm thick flat idols found in these burials, noting that he too had found such idols. Unfortunately, it is not clear from the text whether these latter idols had come to light in Megiddo and if so, whether they had been found in a burial.[188]

The Near Eastern idols recovered from burials are never female figurines depicted with a child, and they are usually associated with sacred prostitution and sexual attraction on the basis of their typological traits. M. Tadmor has

---

[184] I consider this to be the most fruitful approach. Cf. Bánffy 1990–91.

[185] Roaf 1998, p. 56.

[186] Helck 1971, p. 61.

[187] Masson 1968, p. 181.

[188] Jirku 1970, pp. 80–86.

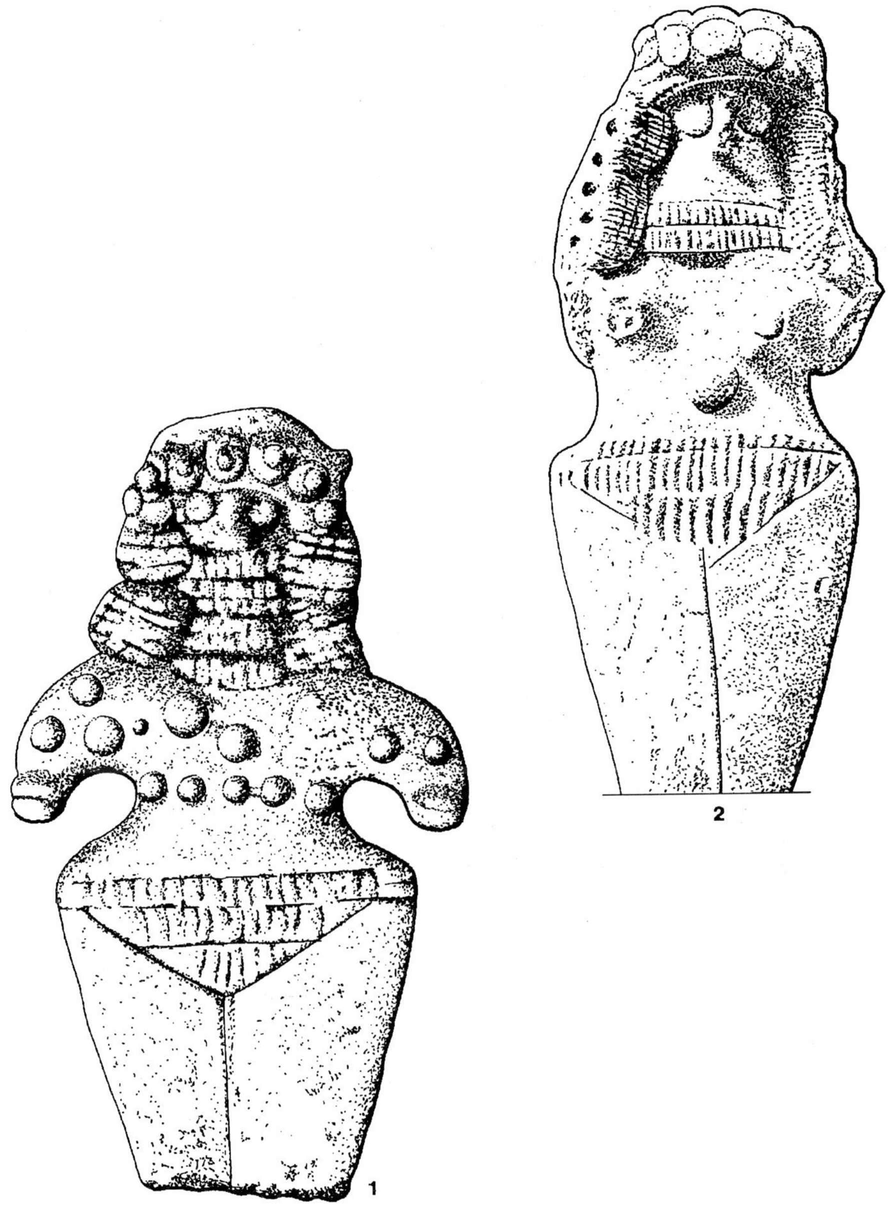

Fig. 25.

1. Tell Asmar (After Müller-Karpe *1974, Fig. 206/23);*
2. Tell Asmar (After Parrot *1962, Fig. 300).*

suggested that the figurines deposited into graves can perhaps be interpreted as substitutes for the deceased's concubines.[189] This suggestion can be rejected on two counts. The available texts do not mention the need for concubines in the netherworld, only the need for some food and fresh water.[190] The textual analysis harmonizes with W. Helck's conclusion based on the archaeological evidence that the graves that contained idols in Cyprus, Egypt, Nubia, as well as at Charchemish and Alaca Hüyük were without exception female burials.[191] In other words, the idols – no matter how emphatically sexual their depiction – which had been deposited in the burials had had some function for the deceased woman; they were perhaps intended to preserve her erotic attraction. According to other sources, the figurines deposited into graves were often only cheap imitations or variants of the statuettes used or displayed in the settlement. For example, the Hassuna settlements of Mesopotamia usually yielded idols carved from marble, while the grave goods were without exception made from clay.[192] Other texts mention grave idols made from various organic or perishable materials, such as wax, bitumen and clay.[193] If the suggestion that the idols deposited in burials were imitations of the idols used at the settlement proves to be correct, it is possible that there was no difference between their function.

(2) Idols from settlements

The majority of prehistoric idols has been recovered from settlements. The large-scale settlement excavations in Central and South-East Europe, begun in the early 20th century, the extensive tell excavations in the Carpathian Basin and to its south have yielded a rich corpus of idols, often as many as a thousand clay figurines from one single settlement. After countless studies on the typology of these figurines, and following many attempts at categorization, the find circumstances and the archaeological context are now also the focus of study. Many of the hypotheses that have been advanced in this field contained

---

[189] TADMOR 19822, pp. 139–173.

[190] TOORN 1998, pp. 93–94.

[191] HELCK 1971, pp. 61–62.

[192] OATES 1966, p. 151.

[193] BLACK – GREEN 1992, p. 81.

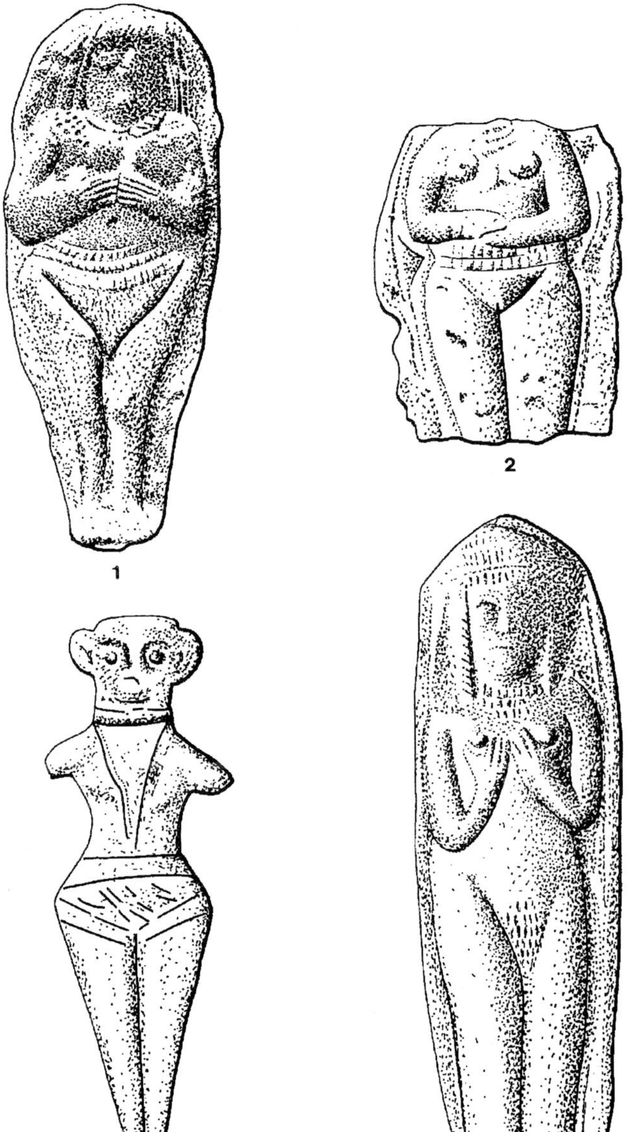

Fig. 26.

1. Mesopotamia (After Champdor *1964, Fig. 74 right);*
2. Tell Asmar (After Müller-Karpe *1974, Fig. 243);*
3. Lachis (After Gressmann *1927, Pl. 99/ 289);*
4. Aleppo (After Bossert *1951, p. 193, Fig. 632).*

grave errors. For example, M. Gimbutas considered every building which yielded one or more idols to have been a Neolithic temple.[194] It later became clear that many of these three-roomed Middle and Late Neolithic 'sanctuaries' were in fact dwelling houses, with a residential room, a room used as a workshop, and only the third room contained finds pertaining to cult life.[195]

It is my belief[196] that buildings which are usually defined as 'sanctuaries' should rather be interpreted as 'community buildings', the settings for certain events – such as initiation rites – affecting the entire community.[197] Finds or phenomena indicating cult life can be demonstrated for each dwelling house, suggesting that the main setting for cult life in South-East Europe was the dwelling house. The cult itself was the private affair of a smaller unit, the family, rather than the entire community.[198]

No matter how the role of clay figurines is interpreted, there is a general consensus that in contrast to the flourishing idol manufacture in the Neolithic and the Copper Age, the decline of the Copper Age[199] saw the virtual disappearance of clay anthropomorphic figurines in the Carpathian Basin, the Balkans and the Aegean; idols re-appeared again only after a long hiatus and only in certain regions, such as the Lower Danube.[200] The Cyclades are an exception, but viewed from South-East Europe, the Cyclades lay on the periphery and it is possible that the flourishing Bronze Age sculptures

---

[194] GIMBUTAS 1980, pp. 41–50.

[195] To quote the examples cited in M. Gimbutas' article (see note 194), the structures excavated at Sesklo (Greece), Cascioarele (Romania) and Achilleion/Farsala (Greece) can be regarded as dwelling houses. Cf. also GIMBUTAS 1989a, Appendix and Chapter 7. Such buildings are often also labelled 'shrines' or 'sanctuaries'. Beside the probable contextual mistake, Gimbutas' usage of the term 'temple' (*templum*) is also erroneous since this term refers to the, non-Christian sacred space or building of antiquity, in contradistinction to the profane settlement environment.

[196] BÁNFFY 1990–91, Chapter 3.2, pp. 205–208; BÁNFFY 1997, Chapter 6.

[197] E.g. the buildings uncovered at Lepenski Vir in Serbia, Nea Nikomedeia in Greece and Nevali Çori in Anatolia. SREJOVIĆ 1969; WARDLE (ed.) 1996, pp. 41–42; HAUPTMANN 1993, pp. 37–69.

[198] P. F. Biehl reached a similar conclusion in his dissertation. Biehl in print. Cf. also BIEHL 1997, pp. 59–67.

[199] The earliest Bronze Age according to the Bulgarian, Greek and Turkish terminology, dated to 2800 BC.

[200] LETICA 1973.

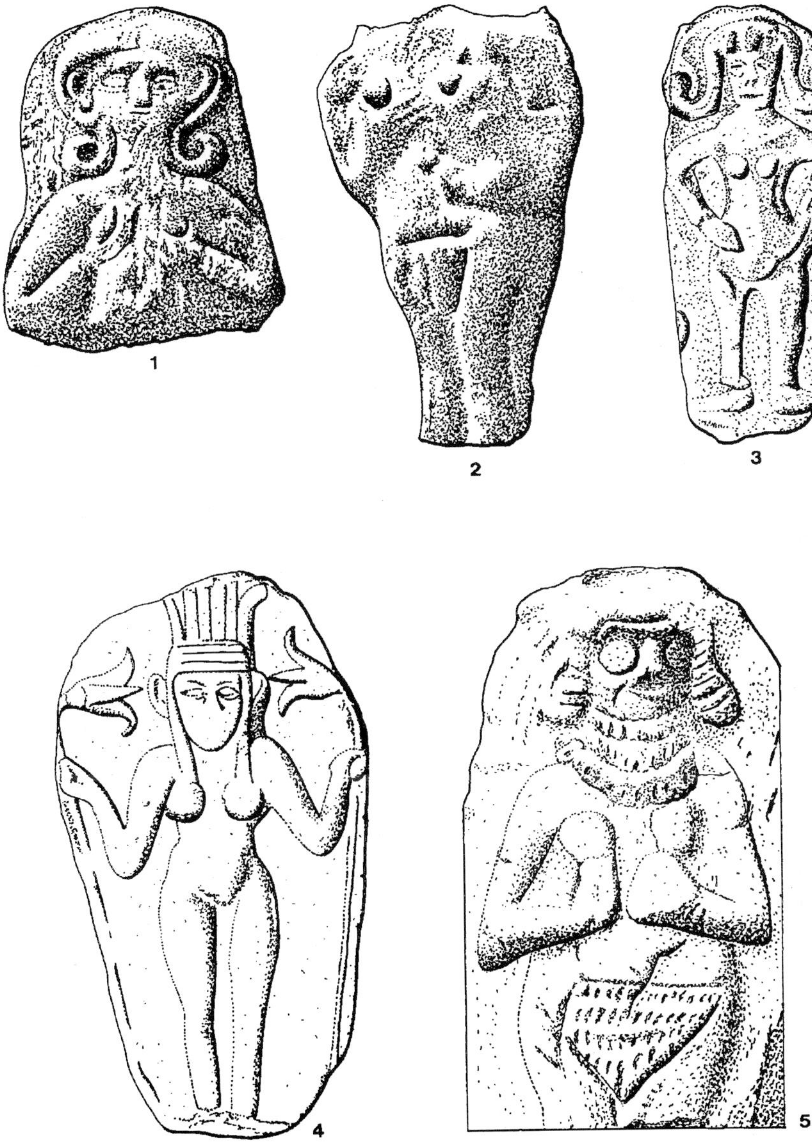

Fig. 27.

1–2. Mesopotamia (After GRAY *1969, p. 70);*
3. Thaanach (After GRESSMANN *1927, Pl. 99/287);*
4. Tell Beit Mirsin (After ALBRIGHT *1949, Fig. 27/5);*
*5. Palestina (*CHAMPDOR *1964, Fig. 70).*

in that region links the Cyclades to the Anatolian and Near Eastern Early Bronze Age, seeing that Cycladic settlements and burials have both yielded an impressive number of figurines.

In contrast to the above regions, no break in cult practices can be observed in the Early Bronze Age of the Near East. A high number of idols were recovered at various settlements, such as Demircihüyük in Anatolia; these idols were associated with some kind of Early Bronze Age religion by the excavator.[201] Hittite sources allow a wide range of possible interpretations for the archaeological finds, and based on these J. Yakar has suggested that the clay figurines and the figurines made from unfired clay, mud and wax had been part of the paraphernalia used in sympathetic magic as documented in these texts, while metal sculptures, such as the figurines from Tell Judeidah in the Amuq Plain depicted various deities. This is also corroborated by the fact that these metal figurines were often buried in the foundation trenches of large sanctuaries or community buildings.[202]

(3) Idols from sanctuaries

Another major difference between South-East Europe and the eastern Mediterranean is that sanctuaries had most certainly been built and used in Anatolia and the Near East by the 3rd millennium BC. Disregarding now the well-known structures in Çatal Hüyük – which, according to the excavator, were not dwelling houses, but Neolithic sanctuaries[203] – the Early Bronze Age double building uncovered at Beyçesultan can hardly be seen as anything else, but a religious structure.[204] Another difference is that countless violin shaped idols were found in these sanctuaries.[205] At the same time, idols have also been recovered from burials and cemeteries in Anatolia.[206] There is a general consensus that in Mesopotamia and its periphery urbanization began at the commencement of the Early Bronze Age, and that the process of urbanization

---

[201] Korfmann 1977–78, pp. 5–59; Korfmann 1979, pp. 187–200.

[202] Yakar 1985, p. 420.

[203] Mellaart 1964.

[204] Lloyd – Mellaart 1966.

[205] Lloyd – Mellaart 1958, Pl. 28.

[206] Kamil 1982, Figs. 284–292.

led to the emergence of fortified towns in which large, massive public buildings – primarily sanctuaries – were built. The appearance of the latter can in part be traced to the fact that cult and religious life, which had previously been the private affair of a family, changed and there was a greater demand for community cults.[207] The development of flourishing urban civilization, however, apparently came to a halt in the last centuries of the 3rd millennium, at the very time when the Budapest idol had been made, the population of the Syro-Palestinian region decreased, many urban settlements were abandoned and nomadic, pastoralist tribes appeared in their stead.[208] These historical events do not facilitate the reconstruction of the possible find context of the Budapest idol. The relevant literature usually studies idols from the perspective of religion, from the Bronze Age pantheon as appearing in the written sources.[209]

(4) Possible relations between the Early Bronze pantheon and idols

In contrast to the high number of idols from settlements and the various descriptions of official religious ceremonies, very little is known about the domestic cults of the population. Regardless of whether they had been found in houses, under the floor, in pits or, more often than not, in a habitation level, idols found on settlements usually came to light together with pottery and other household artefacts. This may very well be the reason that their precise find context often goes unnoticed. It is nonetheless quite certain that in the Near East many figurines were recovered from sanctuaries or temple precincts. A. Spycket has noted that female figurines depicted in the nude were often found in temples and their immediate surroundings.[210] It seems likely that during this period there were, beside closed temples, also open spaces such as groves, where religious life was practised.[211] It is still unclear whether

---

[207] Roaf 1998, p. 73.

[208] Seipel 1997, p. 39.

[209] Kramer 1963, pp. 123–125. with a description of the Sumerian pantheon, together with temples, stone statues and votive artefacts carved from ivory and alabaster, Cf. also van Buren 1930; Badre 1980; Spycket 1981; James 1958.

[210] Spycket 1981, p. 170.

[211] For the variety of sacred places, cf. Eliade 1976, pp. 377–381; for cult practices in groves, cf. Nilsson 1950, p. 272.

the clay idols depict deities, individuals presenting sacrifices, priestesses, or simple people.

The written sources usually contain descriptions of official religious ceremonies conducted by priests, rather than the cult practices of simple people. Data on the religion of the peripheral regions have been preserved in Ugaritic myths, in a few Hittite texts and in the Old Testament, especially in the Book of Kings and Exodus, as well as in Judges and certain passages of Jeremiah and Ezekiel. There most certainly existed an important goddess in the prehistory of the Near East – many of her names have survived, but the frequent fusion between her names reveal that they denote the same deity.[212] In Syria and the earliest Canaanite cults the written sources mention the name Astarte or Astaroth, Asherah and Anat. Anat is often identified with Ishtar and she appears as Baal's consort.[213] Astaroth and Asherah are also mentioned as Baal's consort,[214] suggesting that the different names did not in fact denote major differences between these goddesses. It is possible that the different names served to emphasize different aspects of the goddess: Asherah was perhaps the goddess of fecundity, Astarte of sexuality and Anat of war;[215] still, much controversy surrounds their figures in scholarly literature.[216] This goddess was identical with the Magna Mater of the Ancient Near East,[217] and van der Toorn even speaks of roots in the 4th millennium.[218]

The Syro-Palestinian goddesses, Anat, Asherah and Astarte blended into a single goddess by the mid-2nd millennium: Ishtar, the goddess of love and war.[219] This Canaanite goddess appears in the Old Testament, usually in

---

212 L. Oppenheim describes the process of blending with the following words: "Although fusions created a number of hybrid figures, the names of the constituent deities were nevertheless preserved, yielding a plethora of local and minor deities despite the obvious identity or duplication of many of the names." L. Oppenheim 1964, p. 194. Cf. also a detailed analysis by Blocher 1987, pp. 220 and 222.

213 Gray 1969, pp. 70–74.

214 James 1958, p. 125.

215 Oden 1976, pp. 31–36.

216 Goodnick Westenholz 1998, p. 72.

217 Oden 1976, p. 36 quotes the Song of Deborah in chapter 5 of the Book of Judges, considered the oldest part of the Bible, as "having prehistoric roots".

218 Toorn 1998, pp. 95–96.

219 Gray 1969, pp. 73–74.

passages where the prophets chastise the people of Judah for their sins. In the Book of Kings, the altar erected to Baal and Asherah is attributed to Manasse, while Jeremiah speaks about the sins of the simple people: "and the women knead the dough, to make cakes to the queen of heaven, and to pour out drink-offerings unto other gods, that they may provoke Me."[220] K. van der Toorn has noted that this goddess had originally been Yahweh's consort and that she continued to be worshipped in the Jewish community in Upper Egypt.[221] If the traces of the worship of another goddess and god can still be found in a strictly monotheistic religion, the cult of the Great Goddess can hardly be underestimated in the Near East, both in terms of time or distribution.

Still, it does not follow from the above or from the high number of idols that we are dealing with a Magna Mater cult in the sense that Gimbutas or Bachofen used this term. The worship of the goddess was not necessarily a series of ritual acts performed by women or for women alone, and neither were these acts necessarily associated with fertility alone. J. Goodnick Westenholz has noted that in western cultures women are associated with four values: virginity, chastity, sexuality and fertility – the latter also serving as an excuse for the third. The first two concepts seem to have had no importance in the Ancient Near East, while the latter two were not restricted to women: both males and females could represent them.[222]

The cult of the goddess also reached Egypt, and there is no need for lengthy explanations in view of the historical events, trading contacts and trade routes outlined in the above. J. Gray simply notes that the nude fertility goddess known as Astarte is depicted with the coiffure of Hathor, her Egyptian counterpart.[223] The kindly, but occasionally destructive and dangerous goddess often appears in the form of a cow or with a cow's head.[224] In the Ugaritic

---

[220] Jer. 7: 18, chastising the Jews who succumbed to pagan cults: the men of Judah complain that when they still gave offering to the queen of heaven they lacked for nothing. Jeremiah 44: 17–25.

[221] Toorn 1998, pp. 84–85.

[222] Goodnick Westenholz 1998, p. 64.

[223] Gray 1969, pp. 70–71.

[224] Hassan 1998, pp. 98–112, offers a brilliant analysis of how the goddess came to be depicted in the form of a cow. Hathor's head, depicted with a human face, but with cow's ears and horns appears on the slate palette of Narmer, dated to the turn of the 4th–3rd millennium.

texts Anat, the goddess of love and war, is often described in the form of a cow, indicating yet another link between the goddess worship of these two regions.[225]

Hathor's thick hair, falling to her shoulder in braids on both sides, is not necessarily related to the wide cow's head. There is definitely a link with the highly similar coiffure of Near Eastern idols, and as far as I know, this link has not yet been challenged by any scholar specializing in this field. Loosely falling hair had a special, symbolic meaning in various regions of the world during different periods, and the Syro-Palestinian region of the late 3rd millennium was no exception. W. Helck quotes an opinion according to which hair falling on the shoulders can be associated with child-bearing, although he would rather associate loosely falling hair – especially if coupled with nudity – with erotic love, seduction and sexuality.[226] The fusion of the various names of the goddess can also be noted in Egypt in the 2nd millennium: on the papyri dating from the XIXth Dynasty, Anat appears as one of Hathor's names.[227]

The names of the goddess were not restricted to the few names mentioned here. J. Goodnick Westenholz quoted various Syrian towns from the late 3rd millennium to illustrate the practice of placing a town under the tutelage of a local goddess. The sources always mention the town together with the expression "Lady of ...". The complexity of the Syrian pantheon, or rather, its openness to the reception of deities from other religions, is indicated by the texts from Ebla, which mention forty other deities beside the Sun and the Weather God: eight of these were Semitic (seven male gods and the Sun Goddess), four were Sumerian and ten were autochthonous deities which do not appear elsewhere (five of these were female).[228] The idea of "one town – one goddess" was apparently also a concept shared by the Hurrians.[229] The countless goddess names include also a *potnia hippón*, a mistress of

---

[225] James 1958, p. 122.

[226] The quoted opinion is Brunner-Traut's. Helck supports his own views by citing Egyptian shepherd stories in which the loosely falling hair always characterizes the seductive woman, the 'wanton woman'. Helck 1971, p. 64 and note 38.

[227] James 1958, p. 123.

[228] Goodnick Westenholz 1998, pp. 75–79.

[229] Dussaud 1949, pp. 331–414, esp. p. 340.

the horses, indicating the long ancestry of the goddesses' manifestations.[230] Asherah of Syria is often depicted in the company of various beasts.[231] M. Eliade has noted the "astonishing inclination for religious syncretism" in the early 2nd millennium pantheon of Anatolia: the Hittite pantheon incorporated both the Sumerian-Akkadian deities and the ancient Anatolian and Hurrian gods and goddesses.[232]

The tendency for syncretism, the fusion of cult practices and deities can be of help in explaining the distribution of idol types similar to the Budapest idol at the close of the 3rd millennium. Even assuming that the name and the function of the figurine differed from region to region, the tendency to incorporate foreign ideas into local religious beliefs and practices was characteristic. This phenomenon offers yet another explanation – beside the flourishing long-distance trade – for the appearance of more or less similar idols not only on agrarian settlements, but also among nomadic tribes.

In contrast to the many mentions of the goddess and her countless names in 3rd millennium sources, there are few references to the idols found in settlements during excavations. The Old Testament occasionally mentions graven images made by individuals who succumbed to paganism, which they took into their houses and "served"; in some Biblical passages the name of the graven image is given as Asherah.[233] That these household graven images played an important role is shown by a passage from Genesis. When Jacob abducts Rachel, she secretly packs the *teraphim* from her father's house. Laban accuses Jacob, who had no inkling of the whole business, with the

---

[230] I am here thinking of the *potnia theron*, the Mistress of the Beasts depictions of the Early Neolithic, appearing at Çatal Hüyük and Hacilar in Anatolia. One must be very cautious in identifying the assumed deities of early prehistory with later gods and goddesses, and especially with the gods and goddesses of classical antiquity. There are several cautionary examples in this respect. The one possible exception for assuming a formal and spiritual continuity may be the female figure depicted together with wild animals – lions or leopards – or wearing a garment of these animals' hide that can safely be identified with the Matar Kubile of antiquity or Greek Kybele. For the idols from the above two sites, cf. Mellaart 1975, Chapter 3.

[231] Gray 1969, p. 72.

[232] Eliade 1978, pp. 135–136.

[233] E.g. 2 Kings 21: 7.

following words: "Wherefore hast thou stolen my gods?"[234] When Laban searches for his *teraphim* in his daughters' tents, he is unable to find them because "Rachel had taken the *teraphim*, and put them in the saddle of the camel, and sat upon them. And Laban felt about all the tent, but found them not."[235] This passage suggests that these *teraphim* were important both to Laban and to Rachel and that Laban calls them "gods", and also that these *teraphim* were rather small if they could be hidden under the saddle. Unfortunately, there is nothing to indicate – aside from the occurrence of the name Asherah – that these graven images were female figurines and that they resembled the idols in question. W. Helck is rather sceptical about identifying the graven images mentioned in the Old Testament with the idols, primarily because nowhere is it expressly stated that these images depicted nude figures.[236] For my part, I am more optimistic after a study of the Old Testament passages mentioning graven images, for I believe that the references to the use and place where these graven images and *teraphim* were kept can be reconciled with the archaeological context of idols recovered from settlements – houses and their immediate surroundings. Unfortunately, there are no descriptions of what these graven images looked like and they cannot therefore be compared to the typological characteristics of the idols. Thus the identification of the Biblical graven images and *teraphim* with the idols from excavations is no more than a hypothesis. Household idols, household statuettes of gods or, to use an archaeological expression, idols set up in a special area set aside for domestic cults in dwelling houses can also be demonstrated north of the Syro-Palestinian region. K. Deller has recently demonstrated the presence of the images of deities – statuettes wearing masks – in Hurrian dwelling houses.[237]

Can we assume a link between Laban's *teraphim*, the Great Goddess of the Ancient Near East and the clay idols? Most archaeologists and scholars would deny such a link, although most of them would agree that there must have been some relation between the idols and the worship of the Magna Mater.

---

[234] Genesis 31: 30.

[235] Genesis 31:34.

[236] Helck 1971, p. 67.

[237] Deller 1981, p. 70.

My own answer to this question is no more than a hypothesis. My assumption is that in those periods and in those regions in which the presence of structures, temples or sanctuaries, built specifically for religious purposes cannot be demonstrated – i.e. in the Neolithic and the Copper Age of the Carpathian Basin and South-East Europe – the cult and its paraphernalia were placed in a special area set aside for domestic cults in the dwelling houses. In contrast, there were areas – *temenoi*, sanctuaries and temples – removed both physically and spiritually from the everyday environment in the Near East since the Copper Age. The artefacts, such as figurines, anthropomorphic vessels and house models,[238] which can be associated with cult practices, are usually – although not exclusively – recovered from a settlement context, namely from the settlement or from dwelling houses. In places where the main setting of cult life was the house, the cult itself was restricted to the house and was the private affair of a family, these clay idols and other cult objects were no doubt made by the occupants themselves, perhaps a separate set for each major festivity.[239] The situation in the Near East differed considerably. L. Oppenheim describes in detail the religious ceremonies of the Near East, the everyday activities performed by the priest for the statues of the gods, in which the king and his dignitaries participated during certain festivals. Oppenheim believed that religion played an unimportant role in the life and thought of simple people. They did not participate in the cult, they were mere bystanders, onlookers on religious festivals and community ceremonies. Their "expectations and apprehensions, as well as ... moral code revolved within the orbit of a small urban or rural society."[240] Still, Oppenheim allows that statuettes of deities played and important role in the religion of simple people "as shown by the wide distribution of the cheap copies of such depictions."[241]

---

[238] M. Roaf interprets a house model from the 3rd millennium settlement of Hama as a 'sanctuary model', perhaps in view of the relief depicting birds under the flat roof. Roaf 1998, p. 129. It is my belief that clay models of buildings should not be interpreted as sanctuaries or houses, or perhaps ovens, based simply on their careful or primitive modelling. Cf. Bánffy 1986a, pp. 58–65.

[239] Bailey 1996, pp. 291–295; Bánffy 1990–91, pp. 211–212.

[240] L. Oppenheim 1964, p. 176.

[241] L. Oppenheim 1964, p. 184.

The religious practices of simple people thus took place outside the sanctuaries, which they were perhaps not even allowed to enter. It was therefore only natural that they should feel the need to create their own 'sanctuaries' in their personal environment, to surround themselves and their families with their personal cult objects. The 'sanctuary model' inside the house, the cheap clay copies of the statues of the gods most likely imitated the statues of official religion and served as a substitute for the objects in the sanctuaries, as well as for performing similar rites. These cults were probably very similar, both as regards their content and the objects used, to the Neolithic and Copper Age cult life practised on settlements. Although this cannot be proven, I believe that the Budapest idol and the other similar figurines can be interpreted as an object of this kind: although they cannot be assigned to high art, they were nonetheless carefully modelled and show traces of continuous use.

K. van der Toorn reached a similar conclusion, interpreting the cult objects – primarily idols – found in houses as the substitutes of official cults in the household to which prophylactic powers were attributed.[242]

In any case, there is no major difference between this practice and the religious practices in the Neolithic settlements of South-East Europe and the Near East. There is, however, one major difference between how these objects were made. In Mesopotamia and its periphery, for example in Syria, the idols imitating the statues of the gods were probably not made by the villagers, but by specialized craftsmen working in the sanctuaries. Simple folks who did not practice their religion in 'official places' could buy these figurines near the sanctuaries. This would explain why the same type of idols were found both in sanctuaries and in settlements, in houses or pits associated with houses. The 'sale' of these idols in sanctuaries can perhaps be likened to the devotional objects offered at contemporary Catholic places of pilgrimage, but it would perhaps be more appropriate to cite the example mentioned by Toorn. The Book of Acts recounts that at Ephesus "a certain man named Demetrius, a silversmith" and his fellow silversmiths had a thriving business in the production of miniature shrines of the local goddess, Diana of Ephesus in the 1st century AD.[243]

---

[242] Toorn 1998, p. 94.

[243] Toorn 1998, p. 94.

Viewed in this context, Laban's words, that the *teraphim* stolen by his daughter were his gods, are not as controversial as at first glance. The Budapest idol, with its over-emphasized sexual characteristics, was perhaps intended to represent an aspect of the many-named goddess of the Near East which had little to do with the prophylaxis related to children and child-bearing, but had more to do with the goddess' Anat aspect, with sexuality and love. Obviously, it remains an open issue whether this is an opinion projected back into the past through the filter of current, western traditions and monotheism. What is nonetheless certain is that the possible manufacture of the imitations and cheap copies of the statues of the deities makes any speculation on whether the Bronze Age idols of the Near East were dolls, objects used in sympathetic magic unnecessary.

We may come closest to the truth by assuming that the Budapest idol was a 'copy', an image representing a certain aspect – and by no means the most gentle one – of the Great Goddess. It was not identical with the goddess, since it does not wear a head ornament decorated with horns characterizing the goddess' depictions in official religion, but it was certainly suitable for expressing devotion towards her, and perhaps also for the protection of the house and its occupants.

Imitation, copy or fake?

We have spoken of imitations and copies of the statues of deities. The question is obvious: whether these concepts – which today have rather pejorative undertones – can be applied to these clay artefacts of agrarian religiosity. Can the potter who, instead of the image of Hathor, Astarte or Anat, made these flat 'primitive' figurines with their piercing gaze be regarded as a forger? My answer is negative. Similarly to the statues of gods, the products of official religion which reveal much about the royal and official ceremonies performed in sanctuaries, the figurines made for and used by the people living far from the centres reflect on their world. The result – as shown by the Budapest idol – is at least as characteristic and impressive. The clay idols and house models are relics of a prehistoric art which, in spite of sometimes labelled being imitations, copies of sanctuaries or even 'forgeries' of the original statues of the deities, have a prehistoric and historic significance that is by no means smaller and neither should they be neglected from the viewpoint of art history.

It is to be hoped that we will soon witness the thorough investigation of a 3rd millennium Syro-Palestinian settlement, blending new techniques and common sense – as well as its detailed publication. This publication will hopefully fulfil the role of the devil's advocate, revealing whether the above arguments about the 'orphaned' Budapest idol are also valid for the figurines found in that environment.

Finally, a few words about the possibility of a modern forgery. The fact that the Budapest idol has few, if any, exact parallels does not necessarily mean that the figurine was made in the recent past. As I have tried to prove in the above, although there are several typological traits which can be traced to the eastern periphery of the Iranian plateau, all typological features of the Budapest figurine can also be found in the Syro-Palestinian region, the Bronze Age figurines of the Levant. Even if these traits occur but rarely together on the same figurine – and it is most unfortunate that the closest analogy to the Budapest idol, the figurine in the Brooklyn Museum is unprovenanced – it must nonetheless be borne in mind that these typological traits are only characteristic of the later 3rd millennium, and that neither before, nor after that period do they occur together.

Even if in spite of the above we still believe that this figurine is a fake, we should try to imagine an Arab forger of the 20th century. His primary goal is to make some money, by catering to a demand, as simply and as quickly as possible. In order for our forger to 'invent' this figurine, he would have to have been familiar with many of the studies on archaeology, art history and religion quoted here, as well as with many finds that resemble the Budapest idol, in order to make his fake. Such finds, however, are lacking, both among the published finds, and among the unpublished find types – the scholars to whom I showed the idol or its photograph only offered tentative statements as to its possible cultural affinities. Our Arab forger would certainly fare better by making idols that are found by the dozen.[244] Both dealers and tourists prefer to buy well-known find types since those can be sold more easily.[245]

Let us perhaps assume a well-trained European or North American forger, whom J. Gy. Szilágyi has characterized as an individual "who views his work, jokingly or seriously, as a work of art ... with the firm conviction that 'there must have existed' something like".[246] This latter type of forger could conceivably be an archaeologist and/or a scholar of antiquity, with a thorough knowledge of all excavated and for the greater part unpublished finds, as well as of Egyptian and cuneiform texts. And, we may add, also a gifted craftsman, familiar with the prehistoric techniques of tempering, the use of slips, painting before and after firing, as well as the art of polishing. Such a

---

[244] I would here like to thank Prof. E. Strommenger for her kind help. In her letter she notes that only a few types of Syrian idols are forged and that these can be easily recognized, adding that she has not encountered anything similar to the Budapest idol. I must add in all fairness that she could not confirm my assumption since she did not know of any comparable idols. Prof. H. Hauptmann essentially voiced a similar opinion, noting that although he too had no knowledge of any close parallels, the figurine can most likely be linked to the peripheral regions. I would here also like to thank Prof. Hauptmann for his help.

[245] I would here like to thank Prof. L. Török for calling my attention to this fact. In a recent study, C. Renfrew has also addressed the question of the forgery of prehistoric artefacts, of the damages caused by looting and the apparent hopelessness of curtailing this activity. The bottom line was that he supported collectors. There can be no doubt that collectors who enrich their collections with various items do, more often than not, make them accessible to scholars. Cf. Renfrew 1991. R. Elia, however, challenges Renfrew's views, arguing that collectors cause looting by creating a market demand for antiquities. Cf. Elia 1993, pp. 64–69. What is truly distressing is that in his response Renfrew lays a part of the blame on the scholars who publish these finds. Cf. Renfrew 1993, pp. 16–17.

[246] Szilágyi 1987, p. 5.

scholar would surely have published a series of seminal and insightful studies on prehistoric art and the religion of the Near East.[247] Unfortunately, these works have remained unknown.

The Budapest idol is part of a collection assembled in Egypt, a part of which was eventually purchased by the Museum of Fine Arts. The collector living in Cairo most likely acquired the figurine in the mid-20th century, together with various other Egyptian antiquities. If the figurine had been made at this time, it would surely, to quote J. Gy. Szilágyi again, have revealed something about the age in which it had been made: "this unwitting organic interrelation with the period of manufacture is the main reason for the contemporary success of fakes ... and also for their automatic unmasking in the generations following their creation."[248] Egyptology and Assyriology could look back on a long past by the early 20th century. As shown by the history of research, the main focus of interest lay in the two core areas, the Nile valley and Mesopotamia,[249] while – with the exception of F. Petrie's work[250] – more intensive research in the peripheries, such as northern Mesopotamia, the Syro-Palestinian region, the coastal areas and the Sinai peninsula, as well as the interpretation of the finds reflecting a variety of influences only proceeded from the 1960s (in part owing to the war conditions and the proximity of the military zones).[251] A forger active in this period would have been more likely to manufacture an idol that resembled more closely the sculpture or the figure of a goddess of these two civilizations. In this study I have tried to show the many strands that need to be woven together to fully appreciate the importance and the meaning of this idol. It is my conviction that the Budapest idol has nothing to reveal about the assumed date of its manufacture (forgery), namely of the middle third of the 20th century, and neither does it reveal anything about

---

[247] The possibility that a scholar with such an immense knowledge would prefer to remain anonymous seems most unlikely. "The colleagues' envy is the scholar's only reward on this earth", said Antal Szerb, who was intimately familiar with the inner world of Academe. SZERB 1964, p. 12.

[248] SZILÁGYI 1987, p. 5.

[249] Cf. J. Klima's overview of the history of research. KLIMA 1983, esp. pp. 18–19.

[250] PETRIE 1906. It must here be noted that his work does not contain any figurines even remotely resembling the Budapest idol.

[251] One milestone in this research was the discovery of the royal archives in Ebla in 1975. Cf. BERMANT – WEITZMAN 1986, p. 9.

the earlier periods of research on the Ancient Near East. We can thus almost certainly reject the possibility that the Budapest idol had been made sometime in the mid-20th century or earlier, based on the then known idol types.

Without letting our imagination run too wild, let us conjecture an Arab traveller or merchant instead of the possibilities outlined above. During one of his journeys, perhaps on one of the stations of the millennia-old overland route linking Egypt and Syria, a Bedouin showed him a flat figurine depicting a nude female, which he had found among the ruins of a prehistoric settlement known only to him. The Arab merchant purchased the figurine for a negligible sum and then took it to the first larger town, where there was a flourishing illegal trade in antiquities. He perhaps took the figurine to the shop of one of these dealers and sold it. The idol was then placed on the shelf among the other similar, small finds from Egypt, where it waited patiently for someone to buy it.

Postscript

I first saw the idol published here two years ago in the storeroom of the Museum of Fine Arts. I intended to write a detailed study, but it soon became clear that – owing to the lack of useful data – I could often barely scratch the surface. I have to admit that I soon developed an affection for the idol, even though this remained one-sided. The idol is still in the storeroom of the Collection of Antiquities, lying on the shelf of a glass case. Its brown eyes stare into nothingness, silently guarding the secret of its history.

Acknowledgements

I would here like to thank all my colleagues to whom I showed personally or in letter the photo of the Budapest idol. I am grateful to them all for sharing their ideas with me and for their generous help, and especially to Ildikó Bősze (Frankfurt am Main), Prof. Dr. Harald Hauptmann (Istanbul), Dr. Gábor Kalla (Budapest), Prof. Dr. Joseph Maran (Heidelberg), Dr. James F. Romano (Brooklyn), MA. Magdaléna Seleanu (Budapest), Prof. Dr. Eva Strommenger (Berlin), Prof. Dr. László Török (Budapest), and Prof. Dr. Alasdair Whittle (Cardiff).

Map

Near and Middle Eastern sites mentioned in the text

1. Beyçesultan
2. Hacilar
3. Demirci Hüyük
4. Çatal Hüyük
5. Alaca Hüyük
6. Horoztepe
7. Diospolis Parva
8. Arad
9. En Besor
10. Tel Gath
11. Tel Ma`ahaz
12. Tell el-Ajjul
13. Teleilat el-Ghassul
14. Gezer
15. Megiddo
16. Khirbet Kerak (Beth Yerah)
17. Hama
18. Byblos
19. Ebla
20. Alalah
21. Tell Judeidah
22. Sam`al
23. Tell Bi`a
24. Karkemish
25. Habuba Kabira
26. Chagar Bazar
27. Tell Halaf
28. Tell Brak
29. Yarim Tepe
30. Tell Taya
31. Tepe Gawra
32. Assur
33. Tell Asmar
34. Nimrud
35. Khafaje
36. Eridu
37. Tell Chuera
38. Lidar Hüyük
39. Altin Tepe
40. Tepe Siyalk
41. Kara Tepe
42. Tepe Hissar
43. Turang Tepe
44. Namazga Tepe
45. Djeitun
46. Yanik Tepe
47. Tepe Giyan
48. Susa
49. Tepe Yahya
50. Tal-i Iblis
51. Shahdad
52. Shahr-i Sokhta
53. Bampur
54. Mundigak
55. Quetta
56. Sur Jangal
57. Damb Sadaat
58. Dabar Kot
59. Mehi
60. Kulli

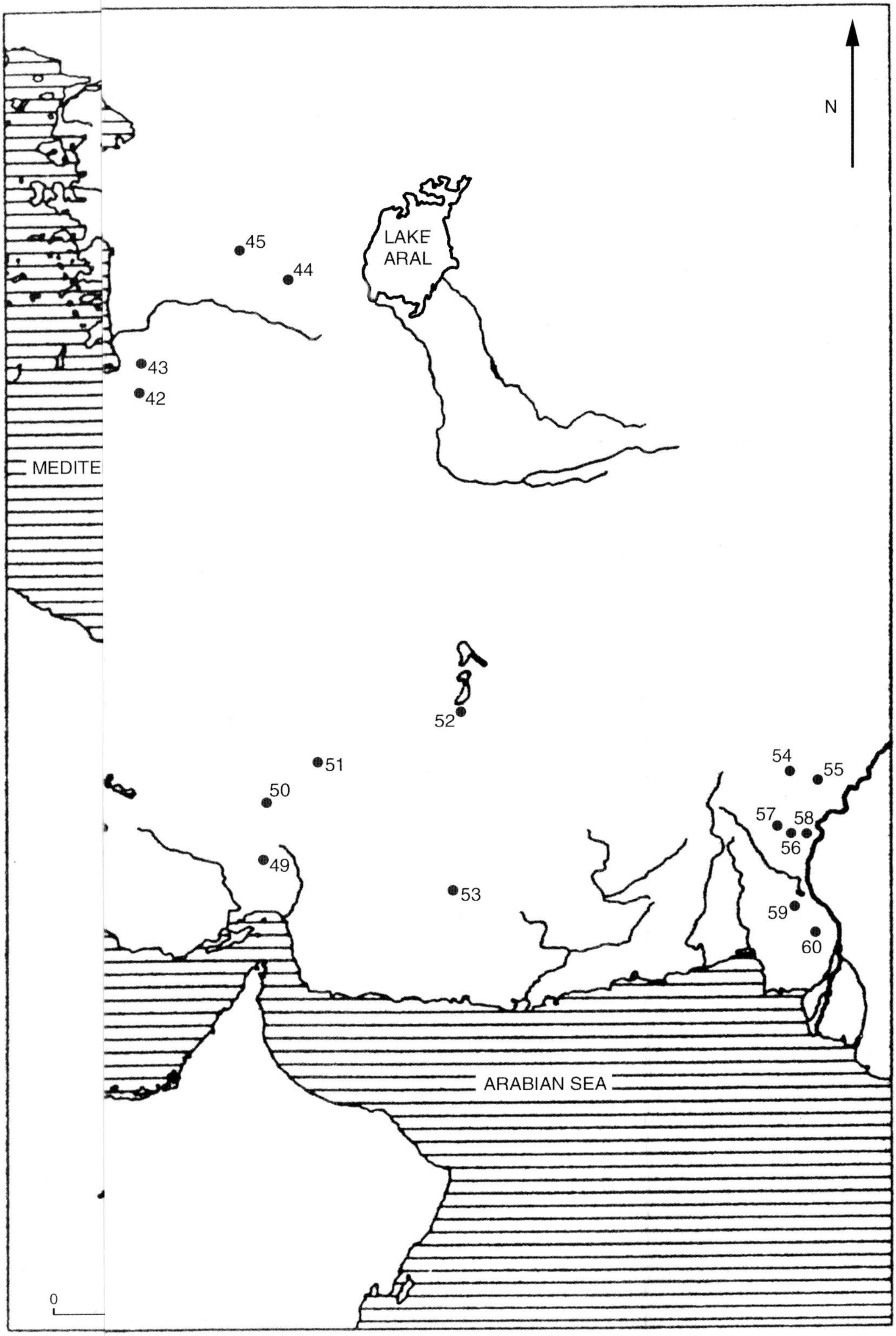
N
LAKE ARAL
45
44
43
42
MEDITE
52
51
50
49
53
54
55
57
58
56
59
60
ARABIAN SEA
0

References

ADAMS, W. Y. 1968

Invasion, diffusion, evolution? *Antiquity* 42, 194–215.

AGRAVALA, V. S. 1965

Indian Art. Varanasi.

ALBRIGHT, W. F. 1949

The archaeology of Palestine. Suffolk.

ALLCHIN, B. – ALLCHIN, R. 1968

The birth of Indian Civilisation. Suffolk.

ALRAM-STERN, E. 1996

Die ägäische Frühzeit. 2. Serie: Forschungsberichte 1975–1993. I. Das Neolithikum in Griechenland. Wien.

AMIET, P. 1977

Die Kunst des Alten Orients. Freiburg/Br.

AMIRAN, R. 1992

Arad. Eine 5000 Jahre alte Stadt in der Wüste Negev, Israel. Hamburg.

ANTONOVA, E. V. 1977

Antropomorfnaja skulptura drevnih zemledeltsev Perednej I Srednej Azii. Moskva.

BADRE, L. 1980

Les figurines anthropomorphes en terre cuite à l'âge du bronze en Syrie. Paris.

BAILEY, D. 1996

The interpretation of figurines: the emergence of illusion and new ways of seeing. In: Hamilton, D., Marcus, J., Bailey, D., Haaland, G., Ucko, P. (eds), Viewpoint. Can we interpret figurines? *Cambridge Archaeological Journal* 6, 291–295.

BÁNFFY, E. 1986a

House models from neolithic Hungary – Attempt at a general interpretation. In: Ucko, P. (ed), *Archaeological »objectivity« in interpretation.* Vol. 2, 58–65. W. A. C. Southampton – London.

BÁNFFY, E. 1986b

Bemerkungen zur Methodologie der Erforschung vorgeschichtlicher figuraler Plastik. *PZ* 61, 152–157.

BÁNFFY, E. 1990–1991.
Cult and archaeological context in Central and South-East Europe in the Neolithic and Chalcolithic. *Antaeus* 19–20, 183–250.

BÁNFFY, E. 1997
Cult objects of the neolithic Lengyel culture. Budapest.

BENAC, A. – TASIĆ, N. (eds.) 1979
Praistorija Jugoslavenskog Zemalja III. Eneolitsko doba. Sarajevo.

BEN-TOR, A. 1981
The relations between Egypt and the Land of Canaan during the 3rd Mill. BC. *AJA* 85, 449–452.

BERMANT, CH. – WEITZMAN, M. 1986
Ebla. Egy ismeretlen ókori civilizáció. Budapest.

BHATTACHARYYA, N. N. 1971
Indian Mother Goddess. Calcutta.

BIEHL, P. F. 1997
Overcoming the "Mother-Goddess-movement": a new approach to the study of human representations. *Archaeology/Latvijas zinatnu Akademijas vestis* 51, 59–67.

BIEHL, P. F. in print
Studien zum Symbolgut der Kupferzeit und des Neolithikums in Südosteuropa. SASTUMA 64. Saarbrücken.

BLACK, J. – GREEN, A. 1992
Gods, demons and symbols of Ancient Mesopotamia. London.

BLOCHER, F. 1987
Untersuchungen zum Motiv der nackten Frau in der altbabylonischen Zeit. Münchner Vorderasiatische Studien IV. München.

BOSSERT, H. 1951
Altsyrien. Tübingen.

BRAUN-HOLZINGER, E. A. 1984
Figürliche Bronzen aus Mesopotamien. *PBF* I/4. München.

BROMAN, V. L. 1958
Jarmo figurines. M.A. degree thesis in the Dept. of Anthropology, Radcliffe College.

BUREN, D. VAN 1930
Clay figurines of Babylonia and Assyria. Yale Oriental Ser. Researches 16. London.

BURNEY, Chr. 1975
Tepe Yahya: its implications for Near Eastern Archaeology. *Antiquity* 49, 191–196.

BURNEY, Chr. 1977
The ancient Near East. New York.

BURNEY, Chr. – LANG, D. M. 1971
The peoples of the hills. London.

BURROW, T. 1969
Dravidian and the decipherment of the Indus script. *Antiquity* 43, 274–278.

CHAMPDOR, A. 1964
Kunst Mesopotamiens. Leipzig.

CHANDRA, M. 1973
Studies in the Cult of the Mother Goddess in Ancient India. *Bull. of the Prince of Wales Museum in Western India* 12, 1–9.

CONKEY, M. – TRINGHAM, R. 1995
Archaeology and the Goddess: Exploring the contours of feminist archaeology. In: Stanton, D., Stewart, A. (eds), *Feminism in the academy.* 99–247. Michigan.

CONTENAU, G. 1914
La déesse nue Babylonienne. Paris.

CSALOG, J. 1959
Die anthropomorphen Gefäße und Idolplastiken von Szegvár-Tűzköves. *ActaArchHung* 11, 7–38.

DALES, G. F. 1960
Mesopotamian and related female figurines: their chronology, diffusion and cultural functions. University of Pennsylvania, PhD diss. Ann Arbor, Michigan.

DANDEKAR, R. N. 1969
Some aspects of the Indo-Mediterranean Contacts. *Annual of the Bhandarkar Oriental Research Institute* 50, 57–74. Poona.

DANNHEIMER, H. (ed.) 1985
Idole. Frühe Götterbilder und Opfergaben. Mainz. Ausstellungskataloge der Prähistorischen Staatssammlung. Bd. 12. Mainz.

DAUMAS, F. 1969
Ägyptische Kultur in Zeitalter der Pharaonen. München – Zürich.

DELLER, K. 1981
Die Hausgötter der Familie Sukrija s. Huja. In: Morrison, M. A., Owen, D. I. (eds), *Studies on the civilisation and culture of Nuzi and the Hurrians (Studies in honor of E. R. Lacheman)*. 47–76. Indiana.

DJAKONOV, I. M. 1981
Evidence of the ethnic division of the Hurrians. In: Morrison, M. A., Owen, D. I. (eds), *Studies on the civilisation and culture of Nuzi and the Hurrians (Studies in honor of E. R. Lacheman)*. 77–89. Indiana.

DUSSAUD, R. 1949
Les religions des hittites et des hourrites, des phéniciens et des syriens. In: *Les anciennes religions orientales*. 331–414. Paris.

ELIA, R. 1993
A seductive and troubling work. On the "Cycladic spirit..." by C. Renfrew. *Archaeology* 1993/Jan.–Febr., 64–69.

ELIADE, M. 1976
Patterns in comparative religion. London.

ELIADE, M. 1978
Geschichte der religiösen Ideen I. Freiburg/Br.

FAIRSERVIS, W. A. 1971
The roots of Ancient India. London.

FRANKFORT, H. 1934
Iraq excavations of the Oriental Institute I. The 1932–33 campaign. Third preliminary report. Chicago.

FRANKFORT, H. 1934–35
Iraq excavations of the Oriental Institute, Chicago. Fifth preliminary report. Chicago.

FRANKFORT, H. 1939
Sculpture of the Third Millennium from Tell Asmar and Khafaje. Chicago.

FRANKFORT, H. – LLOYD, S. – JACOBSEN, Th. 1940
The Gimilsin Temple and the Palace of the Rulers in Tell Asmar. Oriental Institute Publications 43. Chicago.

GAJJAR, I. 1971
Ancient Indian Art and the West. Bombay.

GELB, I. J. 1944
Hurrians and Subarians. Chicago.

GIMBUTAS, M. 1980
The temples of Old Europe. *Archaeology* 33/6, 41–50.

GIMBUTAS, M. 1982
The Goddesses and Gods of Old Europe. Myths and cult images. London.

GIMBUTAS, M. 1989a
Akhilleion. A neolithic settlement in Thessaly, Greece, 6400–5600 BC. Los Angeles.

GIMBUTAS, M. 1989b
The language of the Goddess. London.

GIMBUTAS, M. 1991
The civilisation of the Goddess: the world of Old Europe. San Francisco.

GOFF, B. L. 1963
Symbols of prehistoric Mesopotamia. New Haven and London.

GOLAN, A. 1991
Myth and symbol. Jerusalem.

GOODISON, L. – MORRIS, Chr. 1998
Introduction. Exploring female divinity: from modern myths to ancient evidence. In: Goodison, L., Morris, Chr. (eds), *Ancient Goddesses. The myths and the evidence*. 6–21. London.

GOODNICK WESTENHOLZ, J. 1998
Goddesses of the Ancient Near East 3000–1000BC. In: Goodison, L., Morris, Chr. (eds), *Ancient Goddesses.The myths and the evidence*. 63–82. London.

GORDON, D. H. 1938
The age of frontier terra-cottas. *Iraq* 5/2, 85–88.

GORDON, D. H. 1958
The prehistoric background of Indian Culture. Bombay.

GRAY, J. 1969
Near Eastern mythology. Mesopotamia, Syria, Palestine. London.

GRESSMANN, H. 1927
Altorientalische Bilder zum Alten Testament. Berlin und Leipzig.

HAAG, H. (ed.), 1981
Bibel-Lexikon. Tübingen. Leipzig.

HASSAN, F. A. 1998
The earliest goddesses of Egypt: Divine mothers and cosmic bodies. In: Goodison, L., Morris, Chr. (eds), *Ancient Goddesses. The myths and the evidence*. 98–112. London.

HAUPTMANN, H. 1993
Vier Jahrtausende Siedlungsgeschichte am mittleren Euphrat. *Archäologie in Deutschland* 1, 10–15.

HAUPTMANN, H. 1993
Ein Kultgebäude in Nevali Çori. In: Frangipane, M., Hauptmann, H., Liverani, M., Matthiae, P., Mellink, M. (eds), *Archaeologica Anatolica et Mesopotamica Alba Palmieri dedicata.* 37–69.

HELCK, W. 1971
Betrachtungen zur Großen Göttin und den ihr verbundenen Gottheiten. Oldenburg – München.

HELCK, W. 1979
Die Beziehungen Ägyptens und Vorderasiens zur Ägäis bis ins 7. Jahrhundert v. Chr. Darmstadt.

HIGGINS, R. 1981
Minoan and Mycenean art. London.

HÖCKMANN, O. 1977
The neolithic and bronze age idols in Anatolia. In: Thimme, J. (ed.), *Art and Culture of the Cyclades.* 173–187. Karlsruhe.

HROUDA, B. 1975
Vorläufiger Bericht über die Ergebnisse der 2. Ausgrabungen in ... Isin. *Sumer* 31, 25–32.

JAMES, E. O. 1958
Myth and ritual of the Ancient Near East. London.

JIDEJIAN, N., 1971
Byblos through the Ages. Beirut.

JIRKU, A. 1970
Die Ausgrabungen in Palästina und Syrien. Graz.

KÁKOSY, L. 1979
Ré fiai. Budapest

KÁKOSY, L. 1998
Az ókori Egyiptom története és kultúrája. Budapest 1998.

KALICZ, N. 1981
Die kopflosen Idole der Badener Kultur und ihre südlichen Beziehungen. *Symp. Thracica,* 232–256.

KALICZ, N. – RACZKY, P. 1981
Preliminary report on the 1977–1982 excavations at the Neolithic and Bronze Age tell settlement at Berettyóújfalu-Herpály. Part I: Neolithic. *ActaArchHung* 36, 85–136.

KAMIL, T. 1982

Yortan cemetery in the Early Bronze Age of Western Anatolia. BAR International Series 145. Oxford.

KANTOR, H. J. 1992

The relative chronology of Egypt and its foreign correlations before the first intermediate period. In: Ehrich, R. W. (ed.), *Chronologies in Old World Archaeology.* 3–21. Chicago.

KELLNER, Ph-J. 1982

Gedanken zu den bronzenen Blechvotiven in Urartu. *Archäologische Mitteilungen aus Iran* 15.

KENYON, K. 1970

The archaeology of the Holy Land. London.

KLENGEL, H. 1977

Az ókori Szíria története és kultúrája (Geschichte und Kultur Altsyriens). Budapest.

KLIMA, J. 1983

Mezopotámia. Budapest.

KOHL, PH. L. 1978

The first world economy: External relations and trade in West and Central Asia in the third Millennium BC. In: Nissen, H.-J., Renger, J. (eds), *Mesopotamien und seine Nachbarn. Politische und kulturelle Wechselbeziehungen im Alten Vorderasien vom 4. bis 1. Jahrtausend v. Chr.* 23–31. Berlin.

KOMORÓCZY, G. 1978

Die Beziehungen zwischen Mesopotamien und dem iranischen Hochland in der sumerischen Dichtung. In: Nissen, H.-J., Renger, J. (eds), *Mesopotamien und seine Nachbarn. Politische und kulturelle Wechselbeziehungen im Alten Vorderasien vom 4. bis 1. Jahrtausend v. Chr.* 87–96. Berlin.

KORFMANN, M. 1977–78

Demircihüyük. *Istanbuler Mitteilungen* 27/28, 5–59.

KORFMANN, M. 1979

Eine weibliche Gottheit in der Frühbronzezeit Anatoliens. *PZ* 54, 187–200.

KRAMER, S. N. 1963

The Sumerians. Their history, culture and character. Chicago.

KÜHNE, H. 1976

Die Keramik vom Tel Chuera und ihre Beziehungen zu Funden aus Syrien-Palästina, der Türkei und dem Iraq. Vorderasiatische Forschungen der Max Freiherr von Oppenheim Stiftung, Bd. 1. Berlin.

LAMBERG-KARLOVSKY, C. C. 1972
Trade mechanisms in Indus-Mesopotamian relations. *JAOS* 92, 222–229.

LAMBERG-KARLOVSKY, C. C. 1986
Excavations at Tepe Yahya, Iran 1967–1975. American School of Prehistoric Research, Bull. 38. Cambridge, Mass.

LETICA, Z. 1973
Antropomorfne figurine bronzanog doba u Jugoslavii. Beograd.

LIEBOWITZ, H. 1972
Regionalism in the Art of Syria and Palestine in the Middle Bronze Age. University of Pennsylvania, PhD diss. Ann Arbor, Michigan.

LLOYD, S. – MELLAART, J. 1958
Beyçesultan excavation: fourth preliminary report, 1957. *Anatolian Studies* 8, 93–125.

LLOYD, S. – MELLAART, J. 1966
Beyçesultan I. London.

MALLOWAN, M. E. L. 1947
Excavations at Braq and Chagar Bazar. *Iraq* 9, 1–266.

MALLOWAN, M. E. L. 1954
The excavations at Nimrud. *Iraq* 16, 59–163.

MARANGOU, Chr. 1992
ΕΙΔΩΛΙΑ. *Figurines et miniatures du Néolithique récent et du Bronze Ancien en Grèce*. BAR IS 576. Oxford.

MASSON, V. M. 1964
Srednjaja Azia I Drevnij Vostok. Moskva – Leningrad.

MASSON, V. M. 1968
The urban revolution in South Turkmenia. *Antiquity* 42, 178–187.

MASSON, V. M. 1978
Dzsejtun. Budapest.

MASSON, V. M. – KOROBKOVA, V. I. 1989
Eneolithic stone sculpture in South Turkmenia. *Antiquity* 63, 62–70.

MASSON, V. M. – SARIANIDI, V. I. 1973
Sredneazijskaja terrakota epohi bronza. Moskva.

MELLAART, J. 1961
Excavations at Hacilar. Fourth preliminary report. *Anatolian Studies* 11, 39–75.

MELLAART, J. 1964
Çatal Hüyük. London.

MELLAART, J. 1966

The Chalcolithic and Early Bronze Ages in the Near East and Anatolia. Beirut.

MELLAART, J. 1975

The Neolithic of the Near East. London.

MELLAART, J. 1979

Egyptian and Near Eastern Chronology: a dilemma? *Antiquity* 53, 6–18.

MELLINK, M. J. – FILIP, J. 1974

Frühe Stufen der Kunst. Prop. Kunstgeschichte 13. Berlin.

MERPERT, N. J. – MUNČAEV, R. M. 1981

Investigations of the Soviet expedition in Northern Iraq 1976. *Sumer* 37, 22–54.

MONAH, D. 1997

Plastica antropomorfa a culturii Cucuteni-Tripolje. Piatra Neamţ.

MORENZ, S. 1975

Religion und Geschichte des alten Ägypten. Weimar.

MUNČAEV, R. M. – MERPERT, N. J. 1981

Rannozemledelčeskie poselenija Severnoj Mezopotamii. Moskva.

MUNN-RANKIN, M. 1980

Mesopotamian chronology: a reply to James Mellaart. *Antiquity* 54, 128–129.

MÜLLER-KARPE, H. 1974

Handbuch der Vorgeschichte III. Kupferzeit. München.

MÜLLER-KARPE, M. 1990

Metallgefäße im Iraq I (Von den Anfängen bis zur Akkad-Zeit). *ArchKorr* 20, 161–176.

MÜLLER-KARPE, M. 1995

Zu den Erdgräbern 18, 20 und 21 von Assur. Ein Beitrag zur Kenntnis mesopotamischer Metallgefäße und -waffen von der Wende des 3. zum 2. Jahrtausend. *Jb. RGZM* 42, 257–352.

NEUMANN, E. 1958

The great mother. Zürich.

NILSSON, M. P. 1950

The Minoan-Mycenean Religion and its survival in Greek religion I. Lund.

OATES, J. 1966

The baked clay figurines from Tell es-Sawwan. *Iraq* 28, 146–153.

ODEN, R. A. 1976
The persistence of Canaanite religion. *Biblical Archaeologist* 39/1, 31–36.

OPPENHEIM, A. L. 1964
Ancient Mesopotamia. Portrait of a dead civilizaiton. Chicago – London.

OPPENHEIM, FREIHERR von, M. 1931
Tell Halaf. Leipzig.

OPPENHEIM, FREIHERR von, M. 1935
Tell Halaf II. Leipzig.

OPPENHEIM, FREIHERR von, M. 1941
Tell Halaf IV. Leipzig

PARROT, A. 1962
Sumer. München.

PARZINGER, H. 1993
Studien zur Chronologie und Kulturgeschichte der Jungstein-, Kupfer- und Frühbronzezeit zwischen Karpaten und mittlerem Taurus. Römisch-Germanische Forschungen 52. Mainz.

PEARSON, K. – CONNOR, P. 1967
The Dorak Affair. London.

PERROT, J. 1979
Syrien-Palestina I. Wien.

PETRIE, F. 1906
Researches in Sinai. London.

PERROT, J. 1978
Syrien-Palestina I. Arch. Mundi. München.

PIGGOTT, St. 1950
Prehistoric India. London.

PORADA, E. 1962
Alt-Iran. Kunst der Welt. Baden-Baden.

READE, J. E. 1973
Tell Taya. *Iraq* 35, 155–188.

READE, J. E. 1976
Tell Taya. A summary report. *Iraq* 38, 87–100.

RENFREW, C. 1977
The typology and chronology of Cycladic Sculpture. In: Thimme, J. (ed.), *Art and Culture of the Cyclades.* 59–70. Karlsruhe.

RENFREW, C. 1991
The cycladic spirit: Masterpieces of the Goulandris collection. New York.

RENFREW, C. 1993
Collectors are the real looters. *Archaeology* 1993/May–June, 16–17.
ROAF, M. 1998
A mezopotámiai világ atlasza. (*Atlas of the World Mesopotamia and the Ancient Near East.*) Budapest.
SCHLOSSMANN, B. L. 1975
Metropolitan and provincial styles in Mesopotamia and the surrounding lands in the late third and the early second millennium BC. Columbia University, PhD diss. Ann Arbor, Michigan.
SCHMIDT, E. F. 1937
Tepe Hissar. Philadelphia.
SCHMIDT, R. R. 1945
Die Burg Vučedol. Zagreb.
SEEDEN, H. 1980
The standing armed figurines in the Levant. PBF I/1. München.
SEIPEL, W. (ed.) 1997
Land der Bibel. Schätze aus dem Israel Museum Jerusalem. Wien.
SPEISER, E. 1935
Tepe Gawra I. Publications of the American School of Oriental Research. Philadelphia.
SPYCKET, A. 1981
La statuaire de Proche-Orient. Leiden – Köln.
SPYCKET, A. 1992
Les figurines de Suse I. Les figurines humaines, IVe–IIe Millennaires avant J.-C. Paris.
SREJOVIĆ, Dr. 1969
Lepenski Vir. Beograd.
STAGER, L. E. 1992
The periodisation of Palestine from Neolithic through Early Bronze Age times. In: Ehrich, R. W. (ed.), *Chronologies in old world archaeology*. 22–41. Chicago.
STONE, M. 1976
When God was a woman. The paradise papers: the suppression of women's rites. London.
STROMMENGER, E. 1980
Habuba Kabira. Eine Stadt von 5000 Jahren. Mainz.

SZERB, A. 1964
A Pendragon-legenda. Budapest.
SZILÁGYI, J. GY. 1987
Legbölcsebb az idő. Budapest.
TADMOR, M. 1982
Female cult figurines in late Canaan and Early Israel: archaeological evidence. In: Ishida, T. (ed.), *Studies in the period of David and Solomon and other essays.* 139–173. Winona Lake.
THIMME, J. (ed.) 1977
Art and culture of the Cyclades. Karlsruhe.
TOBLER, A. J. 1950
Expeditions at Tepe Gawra II (Levels IX–II). Philadelphia.
TOORN, K. van der, 1998
Goddesses in early Israelite religion. In: Goodison, L., Morris, Chr. (eds), *Ancient Goddesses. The myths and the evidence.* 83–97. London.
TOSI, M. 1973
Early urban revolution and settlement patterns in the Indo-European borderland. In: Renfrew, C. (ed.), *The explanation of cultural change: models in prehistory*. 424–446. London.
TOSI, M. 1978
The development of urban societies in Turan and the Mesopotamian trade with the east: the evidence of Shahr-i-Sokhta. In: Nissen, H.-J., Renger, J. (eds), *Mesopotamien und seine Nachbarn. Politische und kulturelle Wechselbeziehungen im Alten Vorderasien vom 4. bis 1. Jahrtausend v. Chr.* 57–77. Berlin.
UCKO, P. J. 1968
Anthropomorphic figurines of predynastic Egypt and neolithic Crete with comparative material from the prehistoric Near East and Mainland Greece. London.
UCKO, P. J. 1996
Mother, are you there? In: Hamilton, D., Marcus, J., Bailey, D., Haaland, G. & R., Ucko, P. (eds), Viewpoint. Can we interpret figurines? *Cambridge Archaeological Journal* 6, 300–304.
WARDLE, K. A. (ed) 1996
Nea Nikomedeia I. Oxford.
YAKAR, J. 1976
Anatolia and the "Great Movement" of Indoeuropeans. *Tel Aviv* 3, 151–160.

YAKAR, J. 1985
The later prehistory of Anatolia. The Late Chalcolithic and the Early Bronze Age I–II. BAR International Series 268. Oxford.
ZETTLER, R. L. et al. 1997
Subsistence and settlement in a marginal environment. Tell es-Sweyhat, 1989–1995. Preliminary report. Michigan.

Abbreviations

ActaArchHung	Acta Archaeologica Hungarica, Budapest
AJA	American Journal of Archaeology, Boston.
Antaeus	Antaeus. Communicationes ex Instituto Archaeologico Academiae Scientiarum Hungariae. Budapest
ArchKorr	Archäologisches Korrespondenzblatt. Mainz
Bulletin...	Bulletin du Musée Hongrois des Beaux-Arts, Budapest
JAOS	Journal of the American Oriental Society. Baltimore
Jb. RGZM	Jahrbuch des Römisch-Germanischen Zentralmuseum. Mainz
PBF	Prähistorische Bronzefunde. München
PZ	Prähistorische Zeitschrift. Berlin
SASTUMA	Saarbrücker Studien und Materialien zur Altertumskunde. Saarbrücken
W.A.C.	World Archaeological Congress

Sources of illustrations

1. The whole figure taken from frontside.
2. The whole figure taken from backside.
3. The whole figure taken from rightside.
4. From the head to the arms.
5. Legs.
6. The head taken from frontside to the end of the tresses and the necklace.
7. The head from backside.
8. From the shoulders to the navel.
9. From the breast to the pubic triangle.
10. Ancient Middle Eastern Collection, 72.133. H.: 14 cm. W.: 9 cm. Th.: 2 cm. Baked clay (teracotta) female figurine. Handmade. Late 3rd Mill. BC. Crude, stylized figurine with flattened head. Hair appears as two applied strips on either side of the head; applied flat, circular pellets form eyes, thick short strip for nose. Mouth not represented. The body is nude except for an applied semi-circular strip or "necklace" above applied round pellets or "breasts". Arms extend outward, bent at elbows, forearms placed on above the other on body, just beneath breasts, hand without finger delineation. Below arms, pubic area and lower sides are covered with rows of short, vertical incised lines. The division between the legs is indicated by a deep vertical incision extending downward to feet in the form of small ledges. The back of the figure is flat, with no modeling or applied forms. The clay fabric is buff, green and red in patches. Some areas may have been burnished or painted. Gift of Mrs. Helena Symkovitch.
11.
1. Indus Valley Civilisation. Courtesy of the National Museum, New Delhi (DK 1266/264).
2. Indus Valley Civilisation. Courtesy of the National Museum, New Delhi (H 557/373).

12.
1. Braq. After Mallowan, M.E.L., 1947. Excavations at Braq and Chagar Bazar. *Iraq* 9, pp. 1–266. Pl. 26/3.
2. Braq. After Mallowan, M.E.L., 1947. Excavations at Braq and Chagar Bazar. *Iraq* 9, pp. 1–266. Pl. 26/7.
3. Tell Halaf. Oppenheim, Freiherr von, M., 1935. *Tell Halaf II*. Leipzig. Fig. 56/6.

4. Chagar Bazar/Chabur. After Mellaart, J., 1975. *The Neolithic of the Near East.* London, p. 66, Fig. 101.

13. 1. Turkmenia. After Adams, W.Y. 1968. *Invasion, diffusion, evolution?* Antiquity 42, pp. 194-215: Pl. 28.

2. Namazga Tepe. After Adams, W. Y. 1968. *Invasion, diffusion, evolution?* Antiquity 42, pp. 194-215: Pl. 28.

3. Altyn Tepe. After Masson, V. M., 1968. *The urban revolution in South Turkmenia.* Antiquity 42, pp. 178–187: Fig. 4. above.

14. 1. Tepe Yahya. After Lamberg-Karlovsky, C. C., 1986. *Excavations at Tepe Yahya, Iran 1967–1975.* American School of Prehistoric Research, Bull. 38. Cambridge, Mass. Fig. 7.29.

2. Braq. After Mallowan, M. E. L., 1947. Excavations at Braq and Chagar Bazar. *Iraq* 9, pp. 1–266: PL. 38/1.

3. Altyn Tepe. After Masson, V. M., 1968. *The urban revolution in South Turkmenia.* Antiquity 42, pp. 178–187: Fig. 4. left below.

15. 1. Yarim Tepe. After Merpert, N. J. – Munčaev, R. M., 1981. Investigations of the Soviet expedition in Northern Iraq 1976. *Sumer* 37, pp. 22–54: Fig. 98.

16. 1. Turang Tepe. After Porada, E., 1962. *Alt-Iran.* Kunst der Welt. Baden-Baden:p. 35, Fig. 16.

2. Susa. After Amiet, P., 1977. *Die Kunst des alten Orients.* Freiburg/Br.: Fig. 418, 419.

17. 1. Syria. After Bossert, H. *Altsyrien.* Tübingen: p. 193, Fig. 631.

2. Egypt. After Morenz, S., 1975. *Religion und Geschichte des alten Ägypten.* Weimar: Figs. 19, 20.

18. 1. Northern Syria. After Dannheimer, H. (ed.), 1985. *Idole. Frühe Götterbilder und Opfergaben.* Mainz. Ausstellungskataloge der Prähistorischen Staatssammlung. Bd. 12, Mainz.p. 93, Cat. Nr. 38a.

2. Hama. After Bossert, H. *Altsyrien.* Tübingen: p. 193, Fig. 630.

3. Syria. After Bossert, H. *Altsyrien.* Tübingen: p. 193, Fig. 628.

19. 1. Northern Syria. After Dannheimer, H. (ed.), 1985. *Idole. Frühe Götterbilder und Opfergaben.* Mainz. Ausstellungskataloge der Prähistorischen Staatssammlung. Bd. 12, Mainz.p. 93, Cat. Nr. 44 left.

2. Sam'al. After Klengel, H., 1977. *Az ókori Szíria története és kultúrája (Geschichte und Kultur Altsyriens).* Budapest: Fig. 4.

3. Sam'al. After Klengel, H., 1977. *Az ókori Szíria története és kultúrája (Geschichte und Kultur Altsyriens)*. Budapest: Fig. 5.
4. Isin. After Hrouda, B., 1975. Vorläufiger Bericht über die Ergebnisse der 2. Ausgrabungen in ... Isin. *Sumer* 31, pp. 25–32: Fig. 4.

20. 1. Northern Syria. After Dannheimer, H. (ed.), 1985. *Idole. Frühe Götterbilder und Opfergaben*. Mainz. Ausstellungskataloge der Prähistorischen Staatssammlung. Bd. 12, Mainz.p. 93, Cat. Nr. 44 right.
2. Northern Syria. After Dannheimer, H. (ed.), 1985. *Idole. Frühe Götterbilder und Opfergaben*. Mainz. Ausstellungskataloge der Prähistorischen Staatssammlung. Bd. 12, Mainz.p. 96, Cat. Nr. 42.
3. Habuba Kabira. After Strommenger, E., 1980. *Habuba Kabira. Eine Stadt von 5000 Jahren*. Mainz: Fig. 78.

21. 1. Tell Taya. After Reade, J.E., 1973 . Tell Taya. *Iraq* 35, pp. 155–188.
2. Tell Taya. After Reade, J.E., 1973 . Tell Taya. *Iraq* 35, pp. 155–188.
3. Tell Taya. After Reade, J.E., 1973 . Tell Taya. *Iraq* 35, pp. 155–188.
4. Tell Taya. After Reade, J.E., 1973 . Tell Taya. *Iraq* 35, pp. 155–188.
5. Tell Taya. After Reade, J.E., 1973 . Tell Taya. *Iraq* 35, pp. 155–188.

22. 1. Tell Taya. After Reade, J.E., 1973 . Tell Taya. *Iraq* 35, pp. 155–188.
2. Babylonia. After Amiet, P., 1977. *Die Kunst des alten Orients*. Freiburg/Br.: Fig. 429.

23. 1. Tell Asmar. After Müller-Karpe, H., 1974. *Handbuch der Vorgeschichte III. Kupferzeit*. München: Fig. 206/24.
2. Mesopotamia. After Amiet, P., 1977. *Die Kunst des alten Orients*. Freiburg/Br.: Fig. 430.

24. 1. Tell Asmar. After Müller-Karpe, H., 1974. *Handbuch der Vorgeschichte III. Kupferzeit*. München: Fig. 206/22.
2. Tell Asmar. After Müller-Karpe, H., 1974. *Handbuch der Vorgeschichte III. Kupferzeit*. München: Fig. 206/26.

25. 1. Tell Asmar. After Müller-Karpe, H., 1974. *Handbuch der Vorgeschichte III. Kupferzeit.* München: Fig. 206/23.

2. Tell Asmar. After Parrot, A. 1962. *Sumer.* München: Fig. 300.

26. 1. Mesopotamia. After Champdor, A.. *Kunst Mesopotamiens.* Leipzig: Fig. 74 right.

2. Tell Asmar. After Müller-Karpe, H., 1974. *Handbuch der Vorgeschichte III. Kupferzeit.* München: Fig. 243.

3. Lachis. After Gressmann, H., 1927. *Altorientalische Bilder zum Alten Testament.* Berlin und Leipzig: Pl. 99/ 289.

4. Aleppo. After Bossert, H. *Altsyrien.* Tübingen: p. 193, Fig. 632.

27. 1. Mesopotamia. After Gray, J. 1969. *Near Eastern mythology. Mesopotamia, Syria, Palestine.* London: p. 70.

2. Mesopotamia. After Gray, J. 1969. *Near Eastern mythology. Mesopotamia, Syria, Palestine.* London: p. 70.

3. Thaanach. After Gressmann, H., 1927. *Altorientalische Bilder zum Alten Testament.* Berlin und Leipzig: Pl. 99/287.

4. Tell Beit Mirsin. After Albright, W.F., 1949. *The archaeology of Palestine.* Suffolk:Fig. 27/5.

5. Palestina. Champdor, A.. *Kunst Mesopotamiens.* Leipzig: Fig. 70.

ARCHAEOLINGUA

Herausgegeben von
ERZSÉBET JEREM und WOLFGANG MEID

Main Series

1. **Cultural and Landscape Changes in South-East Hungary. I: Reports on the Gyomaendrőd Project.** Edited by Sándor Bökönyi. 1992. 384 pp., with numerous maps, diagrams and illustrations. DM 140.-. € 71,58. ISBN 963 7391 60 6.
2. Stefan Schumacher: **Die rätischen Inschriften. Geschichte und heutiger Stand der Forschung.** 1992. 292 pp., including maps and illustrations. DM 100.-. € 51,13. ISBN 963 7391 61 4.
3. **Onomasticon Provinciarum Europae Latinarum.** Herausgegeben von Barnabás Lőrincz und Ferenc Redő. Vol. I. 1994. XIV, 364 pp., including maps and illustrations. DM 130.-. € 66,45. ISBN 963 8046 01 5 Ö. ISBN 963 8046 02 3 K.
4. **Die Indogermanen und das Pferd. Akten des Internationalen interdisziplinären Kolloquiums, Freie Universität Berlin, 1.-3. Juli 1992.** Bernfried Schlerath zum 70. Geburtstag gewidmet. Herausgegeben von Bernhard Hänsel und Stefan Zimmer. 1994. 272 S. with numerous maps, diagrams and illustrations. DM 140.-. € 71,58. ISBN 963 8046 03 1.
5. **Cultural and Landscape Changes in South-East Hungary. II.** Edited by Sándor Bökönyi. 1996. 453 pp., with numerous maps, diagrams, illustrations. DM 140.-. € 71,58. ISBN 963 8046 04 X.
6. Garrett S. Olmsted: **The Gods of the Celts and the Indo-Europeans.** 1994. XVI, 493 S. DM 190.-. € 97,15. ISBN 963 8046 07 4.
7. **Die Osthallstattkultur. Akten des Internationalen Symposiums, Sopron, 10.–14. Mai 1994.** Herausgegeben von Erzsébet Jerem und Andreas Lippert. 1996. 588 pp., with many illustrations. DM 200.-. € 102,26. ISBN 963 8046 10 4.
8. **Man and the Animal World. Studies in Archaeozoology, Archaeology, Anthropology and Palaeolinguistics in memoriam Sándor Bökönyi**. Edited by Peter Anreiter, László Bartosiewicz, Erzsébet Jerem and Wolfgang Meid. 1998. 720 pp., with many illustrations. DM 260.-. € 132,94. ISBN 963 8046 15 5.
9. **Archaeology of the Bronze and Iron Age – Environmental Archaeology, Experimental Archaeology, Archaeological Parks. Proceedings of the International Archaeological Conference, Százhalombatta, 3–7 October, 1996.** Edited by Erzsébet Jerem and Ildikó Poroszlai. 1999. 488 pp., with many illustrations. DM 180.-. € 92,03. ISBN 963 8046 25 2.
10. **Studia Celtica et Indogermanica.** Festschrift für Wolfgang Meid. Herausgegeben von Peter Anreiter und Erzsébet Jerem. 1999. 572 pp. DM 240.-. € 122,71. ISBN 963 8046 28 7.

Series Minor

1. Wolfgang Meid: **Gaulish Inscriptions. Their interpretation in the light of archaeological evidence and their value as a source of linguistic and sociological information.** 1992. Second, revised ed. 1994. 58 pp., DM 36.-. € 18,41. ISBN 963 8046 06 6.

2. Winfred P. Lehmann: **Die gegenwärtige Richtung der indogermanistischen Forschung.** 1992. 89 S. DM 36.-. € 18,41. ISBN 963 7391 63 0.
3. Sándor Bökönyi: **Pferdedomestikation, Haustierhaltung und Ernährung. Archäozoologische Beiträge zu historisch-ethnologischen Problemen.** 1993. 61 pp., with illustrations. DM 36.-. € 18,41. ISBN 963 7391 65 7.
4. Ferenc Gyulai: **Environment and Agriculture in Bronze Age Hungary.** 1993. 59 pp., with illustrations and diagrams. DM 36.-. € 18,41. ISBN 963 7391 66 5.
5. Wolfgang Meid: **Celtiberian Inscriptions.** 1994. 62 pp., with illustrations. DM 40.-. € 20,45. ISBN 963 8046 08 2
6. Marija Gimbutas: **Das Ende Alteuropas. Der Einfall von Steppennomaden aus Südrußland und die Indogermanisierung Mitteleuropas.** 1994. Second, revised ed. 2000. 135 pp., with many illustrations. DM 60.-. € 30,68. ISBN 963 8046 09 0.
7. Eszter Bánffy: **Cult Objects of the Neolithic Lengyel Culture. Connections and Interpretation.** 1997. 131 pp., with illustrations. DM 50.-. € 25,57. ISBN 963 8046 16 3.
8. Wolfgang Meid: **Die keltischen Sprachen und Literaturen. Ein Überblick.** 1997. 83 pp., with numerous illustrations. DM 40.-. € 20,45. ISBN 963 8046 17 1.
9. Peter Anreiter: **Breonen, Genaunen und Fokunaten. Vorrömisches Namengut in den Tiroler Alpen.** 1997. 173 pp., with color pictures. DM 60.-. € 30,68. ISBN 963 8046 18 X.
10. Nándor Kalicz: **Figürliche Kunst und bemalte Keramik aus dem Neolithikum Westungarns.** 1998. 156 pp., with many illustrations. DM 60.-. € 30,68. ISBN 963 8046 19 8.
11. **Transhumant Pastoralism in Southern Europe. Recent Perspectives from Archaeology, History and Ethnology**. Edited by H. J. Greenfield and L. Bartosiewicz. 1999. 245 pp., with illustrations. DM 70.-. € 35,79. ISBN 963-8046-11-2.
12. Francisco Marco Simón: **Die Religion im keltischen Hispanien**. 1998. 168 S., with illustrations. DM 60.-. € 30,68. ISBN 963-8046-24-4.
13. Peter Raulwing: **Horses, Chariots and Indo-Europeans. Problems of Chariotry Research from the Viewpoint of Indo-European Linguistics.** 2000. 210 pp., with illustrations. DM 68.-. € 34,77. ISBN 963 8046 26 0.
14. John Chapman: **Tension at Funerals – Micro-Tradition Analysis in Later Hungarian Prehistory.** 2000. 184 pp., with illustrations. DM 60.-. € 30,68. ISBN 963 8046 29 5.

Eastern Alpine Iron Age Studies

1. **Die Kelten in den Alpen und an der Donau. Akten des Internationalen Symposions St. Pölten, 14.–18. Oktober 1992.** Herausgegeben von Erzsébet Jerem, Alexandra Kreen-Leeb, Johannes-Wolfgang Neugebauer und Otto H. Urban. 1996. 462 pp., with many illustrations. DM 130.-. € 66,47. ISBN 963 8046 21 X.

Itinerarium Hungaricum

1. **Pannonia Hungarica Antiqua I.** 1998. 122 S. Itinerary to visiting the visible Roman relics in the Hungarian Pannonia. DM 40.-. € 20,45. ISBN 963 8046 112.

Please address orders to:
ARCHAEOLINGUA
H-1014 Budapest, Úri u. 49.
Fax: (+361) 3758939
e-mail: jer10149@iif.hu http://www.archaeolingua.hu/